Everybody Gets Fifteen Quid

by

Shayne Burgess

Wild Wolf Publication

Published by Wild Wolf Publishing in 2019
Copyright © 2019 Shayne Burgess

First print

ISBN: 978-1-907954-74-0
Also available in e-book

Edited, created, and compiled by Tony Horne.

www.wildwolfpublishing.com

<u>Chapter One</u>

Eye Eye

In 1066 Harold took one in the eye at the Battle of Hastings – so legend and a piece of sewing in Normandy apparently dictates.

In 1964, the story continues. Further arrows were about to be chucked. I, the unknown Shayne Burgess, am born.

There end the similarities. I was not about to sew for starters. Needles were for the beach at Hastings. Plus, this is probably the only detail I retained from school. And nothing, absolutely zilch happened in between those dates. Given that I grew up here and signs were everywhere telling me that some battle took place in a place brilliantly called *Battle* – so not even fucking Hastings – recalling this solitary fact was not much of an achievement.

You might well have the pre-conception that actually, if I threw the darts for a living then obviously I was thick, drunk a bit of beer and was hugely overweight. School would have been something I was probably expelled from. Obviously, some of that is true and some of it isn't. So, let us correct the inaccuracies now. I drank a *shitload* of beer.

I was brought up an only child. Probably, no wonder. Mum

3

Joyce and Dad John surely called time on the whole pro-creation thing when they had me. I am not surprised if they took one look and placed hold on their next order. The family tree confirms: my Dad threw no other darts into my Mum's bullseye.

That said, I had a really happy childhood in a completely different era. Hastings was a run of the mill seaside town but with that iconic status based on something that happened yonks ago. It was pleasant and without trouble but there was not a lot going on. Un-bloody-remarkable probably sums it up.

We lived modestly as most people seemed to do back then but we never went without. Going abroad was out of the question and besides – we were a seaside town that lived through the long hot summer of 1976. Why travel?

But we spent almost no time at all on the front. When you live here, you take it for granted to the extent that you don't bother. I went inland for fun and started fires in the forest. We would get chased by the cops and shoot air rifles for laughs. Messing about in flat lifts was standard. The obligatory throwing things out from high windows not far behind.

That was how you grew up in Hastings.

As you will read, fleeing cops, shooting air rifles and throwing things make the backbone of this story!

I was raised in Kennedy Court, one of the Four Courts high-rise flats. Mum still lives there today. I packed my bags when I turned seventeen. Adjacent to me were blocks named Bevin,

Churchill and Roosevelt. Sussex County Council went through this post-war thing of naming accommodation after Presidents – except of course, Churchill *wasn't* one.

I attended Hollington Infants and then Grove School. Sometimes. Un-bloody-remarkable too and perhaps 'occasionally visited' is better than 'attended'. They never pushed you and I rarely filled a book up. I didn't look up to or idolise any teachers. Mr Boras still haunts me... brutal in Science, smashing your leg with the rubber tube from a Bunsen burner. Back then violence was legal from staff to pupils. Or, so they thought.

I couldn't wait to get out of there. And by the age of fifteen, I did – leaving with no skillset and the assumption that I would be a builder. In fact, my only game plan was to do *something* to earn a crust.

Mum worked in a factory at night. Dad was a builder, 19 years her senior and medically retired. He did well to make a living out of it all having fallen down the tiles one day at just fourteen years old, forcing surgeons to remove his kneecap and leave him with what looked like a wooden leg. His trousers were forever two inches shorter on one side. They had to construct him a build-up a shoe. He looked like a Teddy Boy on one leg!

I am not sure if the roof or my conception were his last erection.

But – there was something in his DNA that just exuded brilliance. I must have taken *something* from it. And I knew it from virtually the age of a baby. Dad was an incredible sportsman. He was totally driven. What I understand now is that he had a focus, an instinct, and a hunger that were almost professional. What I didn't realise at the time was that they were real qualities. He was just my Dad – a scratch golfer and playing darts in the local league at least twice a week. Ordinary bloke in the street who could play a bit.

Except he wasn't. He was better than that. But because he had no greater ambition and the paths to potential glory were not as mapped out as they are today, I do not know how good he really was. Yet I do recognise that without his passion and also self-centred bloody-mindedness, I would not have picked up an arrow myself. Unless I had wandered into one of those stupid *battle* re-enactments at Battle Abbey that take place every now and then.

Mum toiled in the factory. On the nights Dad went out to play darts, I sat in the car waiting! Yep, back then kids were not allowed in the pubs of Britain but their own fathers were allowed to play darts all night, take a packet of crisps out to their son waiting for five or six hours with just colouring books for company and then drive him home well after closing time, half-pissed and half-broke.

His days roofing were over but his nights on the tiles had just begun.

Dad *was* good though, brilliant at every sport he turned his

6

hand too. If he wasn't making you looking a dick on the golf course, he was sticking the pink right up on your arse on the snooker table. He was amazing at every individual sport involving some sort of prop. He just loved victory. He even found himself into the annals of Hastings history, which had been pretty much blank since Harold succumbed, by becoming the only person to win the internationally renowned Town Cup for golf two years on the spin. I am pretty sure if you wander through Hastings today, just past the signs for Bexhill after the William The Conqueror gift shop, you can see the Heritage plaque marking this key event in Sussex's history.

Can you fuck?

Nor to the point is there a William The Conqueror gift shop.

Dad was a builder who lived for sport, much better at golf too than he realised. But back then, you *wouldn't* know. Scouting and broadcasting of any event were so rare. If you made it, beyond your actual skill, there was a lot of luck involved.

He was a proper man's man, smoking and drinking and fitting every stereotype of a bloke from yesteryear.

He was a sportsman who almost didn't live at home – usually out at 0430 before sunrise to play eighteen holes at dawn before playing another nine at dusk. I would often only see him during the day at weekends. He was always playing a round without playing around.

On the rare occasions that he was there, something was

already embedded in the sub-conscious. I suppose it was actually pretty blatant that if he left you in the car twice a week while he went in to shoot some darts, you might actually wonder what it was all about. Plus, there were the trophies – he had pots of them. That was the level of obsession. But he was single-minded and single-focussed. When he was playing darts, he wouldn't touch the golf – and vice versa. It was one or the other. So, he went years without picking up an arrow or likewise a club, but he always had some sort of sporting equipment in his hand.

Apart from that, I retain few childhood memories. Perhaps I only recall Dad's sporting prowess *generally* because of its influence on me. Or possibly my friend Stella had just eroded the mind. Not a great admission less than 2000 words in your memoirs!

I do remember Mum and Dad going for picnics – quite a post war thing to do in a seaside town. They would sit there and lay out the blankets and pretend to be romantic eating their sophisticated Scotch Eggs and I would just head back to Dad's car knowing that he kept his darts in the glove box and just ping arrows at one of the many trees in the forest.

I wasn't very good but there is clearly a beginning there. Dad had rubbed off on me. With no training I had picked the things up. Suddenly, I was having a go, seeing what all the fuss about. Plus, I hated Scotch Eggs.

Somehow, I formed a habit. It was either in my genes or I

had just acquired the trait from being surrounded by it all the time. The smoking working men's club gave Dad an outlet and me, ultimately, a career.

Frankly, I was useless at everything else. At the age of five, I had fallen off a wall and completely smashed my eardrum…the doc said I would never be any good at sports. Of course, being deaf from that point in one ear meant that I never heard him.

Pretty good news really – because I turned out to be rather good at the sport of darts.

Chapter Two

Limp Dick

Good old Mr Limerick never knew that we were taking the piss all that time. He was our Maths teacher and you were supposed to almost swallow his name when announcing it so Limerick became Lim-Rick and from that the Limp Dick emerged!

To his credit and his idle penis, Limp Dick rose to the occasion. For some reason, he let us organise a darts tournament after school and we ended up staying later and later every night for about six weeks before that particular phase passed for most of our gang.

Limp Dick thought it would help our Maths. He then enlisted the Metalwork and Woodwork classes' assistance to make trophies. Nice idea. Nothing was going to improve my skills in that department.

I had opted for Home Economics instead of building shite so I wasn't responsible for the glamorous silverware on offer. Everyone's Dad seemed to be in construction so I thought I might as well learn to cook.

But it wasn't *my* Dad who got me hooked despite all those middle of the week car journeys to dark and dingy pubs. He was going through his golf phase by the time I turned fourteen and had packed up the arrows. It was my best mate from school Mark Card and his Dad Keith who really led the pack. Keith was a very good player and it was rubbing off on his lad. I had become friends with Mark and before I knew it was addicted.

Suddenly I was reading third hand their passed-on copy of *Darts World* magazine. I devoured all the write-ups on the Counties Scene and read the interviews with the few professionals that there were thinking this was some sort of one way ticket to paradise. I learned that you *could* actually make a bloody good living from darts but the most likely place to do so was by winning at venues like *Pontins* and *Butlins* of all places. There was a massive holiday camp scene – probably not the worst idea in the world either to have something sharp and pointed in your hand in amongst all that Hi-de-Hi forced bollocks!

When they ran a piece with the big Welshman, the late Leighton Rees, who went on to be the first ever World Champion, I was in awe. I had found my first hero too in Jocky Wilson and – what seems crazy now – soon was heading off to London to buy whatever the latest fad was on the scene. Darts shops were thin on the ground on the South Coast. The nearest to home were Frank Johnsons in Brixton or Jerry's in Wimbledon. If you saw a new set of flights in the mag, then you got on the train to get them.

Never mind girls, and cars and pop music. I needed to shoot that poison arrow.

So, the three biggest influences were my *golf* mad Dad, Mark and Keith Card, and some Maths teacher who broke every Health and Safety rule in the book.

Limp Dick too had soon had enough. Frankly, there was no improvement in our arithmetic. In fact, we took that less seriously because we knew that after the school day, darts was coming. So, we were always on a countdown. My other friends outside of Mark also moved onto something else in no time at all and bullseye after hours soon became a thing of the past.

Limp Dick had risen briefly only to flop again.

He had made an impression, though. I used to have to bunk off school to watch the only darts show on TV, *The Indoor league* with the former cricketer Fred Trueman which showcased games played in pubs and for some reason was screened in the middle of the afternoon as a housewife's favourite! Kids – we didn't even have video recorders then let alone iPlayers! It doesn't exactly sound an award-winner does it but between 1973 and 1978, Yorkshire Television made it into legendary stuff. And that was it for your fix of darts. The chances of anybody taking it up were therefore pretty slim.

If your Dad played, you couldn't get in the pub. If you were looking for it on the box, you had as much chance of dear old Fred equally playing shove ha'penny on telly. But more to the point, not every school had a limp dick.

Come to think of it, they probably did.

But the age of fourteen marked a turning point. Dad's single-mindedness rubbed off on me. I was hooked overnight. I had one real option if I wanted to pursue this thing. It was time to wreck the hell out of the only place a darts board would fit in our flat...Mum and Dad's living room door.

Chapter Three

One Old Banger To The Next

Mum and Dad's lounge just about held on. Soon, they could see it was worth it. As parents, they recognised that if I took something seriously, then they would be very supportive.

Come to think of it, that's a lie because I had never applied myself to anything up to this point. The truth was that even at an early age, this was the only thing I ever devoted myself to. They were already in the last chance saloon! Somehow therefore, they managed to smile against the continuous backdrop of the thud into the wood of the door and the permanent little holes that are still there to this day. They must have thought they were clutching at straws whilst I was clinging to arrows.

I hope that Dad surely had a sense that I was reasonable. All he had to do was look in the mirror and see that I was just copying him but with my own influences.

And by the age of fourteen, I had come second in a shootout at the *Welcome Stranger* pub. I lost to … Mark Card's Dad but he obviously could see that I had made an impact because he gave me the £30 prize money and the tin-pot trophy. To a fourteen-year-old that was a lot of money. But more importantly, it was also an early marker as to what lay ahead in competitive darts – fuck all money and a shit piece of silverware!

Keith, Mark and I continued to play but Mark later drifted towards settling down to a family life. It happens at that age. I don't know because obviously I am the better looker! We did re-unite some years later for the story of all stories to dine out on in family banter. We were to find ourselves playing in a League Pairs Final where I partnered Keith and my Dad (back throwing again) was with Mark. We won of course therefore creating the ultimate put-down for a million conversations. Nobody would ever forget who won that night and nobody would ever let them do so. The story was on endless repeat.

Seeing less of Mark, I started hanging around a boozer called *The Comet*. This was my first bad career move. I went through a Dad like moment and started playing pool – only because my mates were. I began to hit the ale and gave up darts until I was close on 20 years of age.

Looking back, these are the years when young sportsmen really kick on. Now, even though some of you might think darts is not fitness-based and these are not formative years for the future pro, those adolescent years form habit and I took the game right out of the equation.

In fact, the only preparation for a career in it was that I learned to drink.

But I swapped the bullseye for the green blaze and watched all my mates turn up in their shoddy second-hand snooker waistcoats with their own cues in narrow black boxes like they were the real deal, and I just went along with it.

I take one thing from my time at the table. I clearly had a skill that highlighted good hand to eye co-ordination. But I didn't have the attitude. In fact, I had an attitude all of my own!

So disinterested was I that one night I provoked a massive row on the final black. Under local rules, you had to nominate a pocket to pot the last ball. My opponent smashed the black towards the far right and rattled the jaws, serving me victory on a plate. It was game over once I had completed the formalities. It was so close to being potted that frankly if someone farted, it would have gone down.

'Which pocket are you nominating?' the ref asked.

'Don't be stupid,' I replied.

'You must nominate which pocket,' he re-iterated.

So, I ignored him and rammed it home.

The ref awarded the game to the other team because I had not declared the obvious. As you will read, 'local rules apply' will come back to haunt me time and time again.

I went mental, shouting that they could all fuck off and threw my cue down announcing that I would 'never play this stupid game again'.

It was obviously a pivotal moment and maybe it had been

brewing. Quite possibly, it was nature's way of saying 'get back on the darts board'.

I stormed round the other side of the bar and slammed my glass down in front of the landlord Mervyn. I hadn't even thought about what I was saying.

'You got a darts team?' I asked. 'I am not playing pool anymore.'

'You won't get in it,' he replied. 'We are top of the league.'

So that was that. Door slammed shut. Then I had a thought.

'I don't care if I have to chalk every week, put me down,' I told him.

Two weeks later at the end of that night's match, there was The Gallon...one leg of 1001. I threw a maximum. I went straight into the team and was never out of it again.

I realised for the first time – and maybe it had taken the years away potting to do this – but I was actually quite good. I had a bit of clarity and self-analysis. I knew it was time to rack up some miles and shoot some serious darts.

I had to earn a living too. From school, I had gone straight onto a government YTS scheme meaning that I was raking in a massive £25 a week for Monday to Saturday. I was on my way to becoming a trainee butcher.

Never mind bloody Harold – that is a piece of history in itself, isn't? The government were providing apprenticeship schemes. Professional sportsmen learning a trade and going back

17

to it on a Monday after a weekend at their game. Proper old school, having left school.

From there, I collected glasses at the Coombe Haven Holiday Park. Clientele: permanently pissed. I didn't last long – fired for throwing a box of crisps into an array of lights which came tumbling down.

After that I was back in amongst the meat at Busses Sausages. I had literally gone from camp to mincing.

I can't even begin to imagine how I stuck it out there – there was one saving grace. The canteen had a dart board and we got an hour for lunch. I was in there for 59 minutes every single day.

I had little alternative. The sport had consumed me, and school and myself had rejected each other. The only thing I had been good at was cooking and even then, I got thrown out of class. We were supposed to make Dundee Cake one week and bring in all the ingredients from home. I realised one thing in my final year – that soon I would be working and would need to cook. So, I told her:

'I want to learn how to cook,' I ranted. 'You know…proper stuff like bacon and eggs. When I come home from a hard day's work, I don't wanna be eating sodding Dundee Cake Food for tea.'

She took my point on board.

'Get out of my class and don't come back,' she responded.

Food would, in later years, become a massive part of me – so

18

to speak. Yet still the rules and structure of the classroom killed me and I didn't care a jot if I bunked it, was placed on report and went home to cook myself. I knew it was only a matter of time before I was out of there and moving on to better things. And that meant I became king of the sausage factory!

But of course, when your job is as shite as that and even though you are actually making some cash, albeit a pittance, you are going to take every opportunity to find a game.

One Sunday, Dad Finally took real notice, and issue. I had turned up at The Tivoli Tavern in Hastings where everyone put a quid in to play a game called *Halve It*. When I walked home with a tenner in my pocket, Dad was all over me like a rash asking where I had got it. He had won nothing at golf that day and his 20-year-old son had just returned home with the darts takings from the pub!

I think it triggered a few reactions in him. Firstly, the boy could play. Secondly, the lad had come back with winnings when he had a shocker on the greens.

I swear it must have woken him up because some weeks later he never played golf again until later life. All those trophies and all those hours when he had abandoned family life just hit home in that moment. Suddenly, his son was repeating the cycle but might actually be a bit better. It irritated him too because as an amateur golfer you were not then allowed to win money.

He was impulsive and bloody-minded and sold his clubs on

19

the spot. I don't know if he was pissed off that I suddenly was making cash when he had all those trophies but no financial reward or if he came to that father-son moment that we all do when you stop dreaming you are going to be a sports star yourself and instead channel it through your kids!

I nicked him a set of darts from the pub, the board went up at home again and he practised every day for eighteen months. Then from nowhere one Sunday he announced 'I'm ready. Let's go up the pub.'

Game on. Dad was back.

A year and a half's worth of 'training' all because he had seen me win some money when his scratch golf rewarded him with nothing. Of course, he walked home with the takings from The Tivoli at the first attempt.

The old fella was suddenly the new kid on the block.

For once, I had serious competition – except I still to this day do not know how good he was. I could see him demolish all and sundry yet he would never beat me. People tell me he was the better player. I think he stood aside to encourage me. He was probably, therefore at least the better man.

In four years at the bloody sausage factory, I surely annoyed the hell out of everybody there. I knew I was improving all the time and yet I must have been infectious in either a good way or a bad one. They have been focussed on their chipolatas but all I could thing about was making mincemeat out of my next opponent. Life became a mission to play every night and find the next tournament after that.

For somebody who had shown no drive at anything in life, suddenly it had arrived in bucketloads. Not only did I somehow find the mental strength to get up and deliver sausage after sausage after late nights on the oche but in between darts and bangers, my nervous energy was always visualising the bullseye.

I probably was not the guy to be operating slicing equipment when my mind was elsewhere.

So, I would be up at six and work until three, always dreading Sunday nights at returning to the routine and that mundane normality meant watching the chopper dissect meat into liquid at twice the speed of sound and waiting for the sausage to come out the other end. I was on the 'guillotine' to check the frozen meat going into the sausages. It was a shit job with shit pay. But, my drive had kicked in so much that in the night, now living in my bedsit, I would wake every couple of hours, play darts for 90 minutes and then go back to sleep. I was obsessed with pushing myself and getting better all the time.

I loved the adrenaline of it. Equally, I knew it was all I could do.

Some sort of self-awareness hit me that to improve, I had to meet better opponents. In Sussex, we were not playing with the big boys at all. From the knowledge I had acquired from pub talk and reading *Darts World* for so long, my instinct told me to stop being a silly sausage and get down the road to Surrey, Hampshire and of course, London. You have got to play better players to get *better*.

So, I saved up my huge earnings from work and invested in a car! Dare I say it ...an old banger. Being the king of style and aware of my future image rights, I handed over 300 good notes ...for an old Lada. We will overlook the fact that I had no driving license. I could see nothing but possibilities ahead as I dreamed of swapping Cumberland for Wonderland.

__Chapter Four__

Eat, Sleep and Drink Darts,

Minus The Sleep Bit

Rules were different then. The cops also turned a blind eye. Your bobby on the beat liked to give you a ticking off but rarely got his notebook out for much more. So, I taught myself to drive!

London's Super League was on a Monday night and once I had clocked off at the sausage parlour, I hit the road for the Big Smog, down a gut full of beer and get back home for 2 a.m, only to rise again to pound my meat (so to speak), knowing that unlike the sausage I was on a roll and that if I could make it, the Wurst was definitely behind me.

That is why I needed a ghost-writer – to come up with shite like that!

On Tuesdays I would be back towards the capital for darts in Walton-on-Thames in Surrey. This is where the posh people lived but where serious arrows were thrown. On a Wednesday, I would be back in Sussex for the not so super Super League and by Thursday I would be thinking I was half way to writing a fucking Craig David song without all the rhyming and all the women.

In fact, come that point in the week, I was so knackered that I would go to bed with my clothes on, not even stopping to take my boots off. Darts was out of the question. But, of course, I knew the weekend was coming and that the small matter of bashing out a sausage would pass for a couple of days, so a day of rest was simply only about getting fired up to go full kilter for the weekend.

Invariably, my mate Gary Lawrence who had moved down from London, and I, would get to his pub The Granville early to practise, even though I all I did ever was practise. I even visualised the fucking sausages as arrows to get me through to knocking-off time and just like anyone who has worked the factory line, those last 60 minutes every single day were a daydream where you slipped in and out of consciousness on auto-pilot churning bangers but in fantasy land banging out darts.

My aim every weekend was simple. Wherever I thought I could win a tournament, I would go.

I had a vision. Every day was about every night and that only meant one thing. Survive on minimalistic sleep and get to the oche. Every pound of mince I saw was simply a pound to spend on fuel and drink. I say this taking the piss but I knew I had to get out of the sausage game.

I literally threw everything at it, and of course, even when you are winning, you still don't really know how good you are or if indeed you are any good. Of course, you can recognise the

24

chancers from the real serious players on the circuit but there is a massive gulf from winning one night in a pub to coming second in another. You have to do the hard yards time and time again. Everybody starts this way – shooting arrows in between pints – but it does not breed consistency and then when you start to win regularly, you almost have no edge because it is too easy and too often and if you do slip up, there are no consequences bar a long drive home beating yourself up and replaying that double you missed. You get to a point where you have seen off everyone more than once. Testing yourself after that becomes the challenge.

Suddenly in 1985, it got serious. Gary asked me to play Pairs with him for the Sussex Play-Offs in the British Gold Cup. We qualified for the next stage.

I use the word suddenly and it sort of implies an overnight success but nobody achieves that. Any journalist can print shite like you 'burst onto the scene' but it is my Mum and Dad's flat, Limp Dick's plastic trophy, sleepless nights getting up to practise *and* the years on the green blaze lost to darts that mean there is no suddenly about it. The suddenly is only in the realisation that you can do it. And it takes a tournament win to make you believe.

So I had packed up the old Lada and headed for the Las Vegas of the North...or as it's known in Stoke, Stoke. All roads led to the finals at The Trentham Gardens Gold Cup – a trophy clearly right up there with the Jules Rimet! It shows how amateur darts literally was. I was burning fuel and cash just to even get there. Sometimes I nicked money just to make the venue. But something drove you on. Seeing your name on the line up at a 'major' tournament was a spur of ambition that overrode financial gain and fame. You knew you were playing for fuck all, so you had to be playing for something else. If you could cover your costs, you had hit the bullseye but realistically you wanted everyone to know that you *were* the new kid on the block and they should stand aside. You were coming through.

Gary and I gave it everything only to lose in the final to Peter Taylor and *Shady* Lane. To this day, I still don't know Shady's real name and I can't ask him as he is no longer with us. We played bloody well and even though we were gutted to lose, I did of course realise that I could play just as well on the big stage as on the floor.

But there was no link to a professional darts body, no route map to success, no 'career path'. It was just a tournament here and a venue there. The chances of you making a name were fine within the circle of players and tournament organisers but to a wider public, sponsors and national fame, there was no structure. You still drove yourself to a shitty fag-stained venue full of pissed-up meatheads and then got yourself home with a few quid or not in your pocket. The concept of professional sport was a million miles away, as was the game-changer in satellite television. If I am honest, it was a shambles, something to be embarrassed about in the modern era where every layer of anything resembling sport is scrutinised from an early age of kids being scouted almost before they can walk in the belief that they will kick a ball for Manchester United when they never will. *We were in a make it up as you go along culture.*

But you only think of it in these terms now. All I did was drive every fucking inch of the motorway to live my dream and only the passing of time and Sky TV has made me realise that even though I was living the dream, it was a fucking nightmare really.

Chapter Five

1984

I remember at school being forced to read a book by some cunt called George Orwell. I have no idea what it was about – a few pigs and communism was all I retained. It didn't do me any harm.

Growing up of course, every kid was aware that 1984 was meant to be a doom year. The world was probably going to end or something like that and nobody I knew had really read that book but through ignorance, word had spread that that particular year was going to be hell on earth.

As we all know 1984 was bollocks. And forgive me for not having the same literary skills as George Orwell, but without 1984 I could not have got to 1985 and that first tournament.

You see, just one year before, albeit at this stage as a fan who could play, Kevin Ling, Dean Stanbridge, Paul Greenaway, Dave Adams and myself hit the road jack.

'Can we go to Jollees,' I asked Dave, 'to watch the World Championships?'

I had never been to an event. Jollees was a cabaret-cum-nightclub venue so obviously the perfect location for the biggest tournament in the game! The only darts I had seen live were when I was waiting to play from across the bar. I wanted to taste the big time in the very small not very big, big time. I guess I knew that the stars that we would be watching were players I had dreamed of being but also wondered if I could dream of beating.

I wanted to be in touching distance. But I was also a fan. I couldn't dream that one year later, I too would be rocking up in Stoke! Especially as in 1984, none of us had a fucking driving license. George Orwell might have driven the agenda but none of us could drive on the road.

It was, of course, that different era that I mention often. Nor did you worry about small details like that. Dave knew a bloke called Colin. Colin lent us a driving license. Together we hired a vehicle. We chipped in to get a classy Sierra. The plan was to have an adventure. Paul Greenway was just about the most competent of the non-drivers. Stoke, here we come. Paul, you are at the wheel.

We had no money whatsoever and we were all sleeping in the car. Things were so tight we would drive around the car parks at night with a petrol can, siphoning off fuel to get us around.

We were also wide-eyed – and occasionally legless. People did not travel even back then in 1984. The country was ripped apart by industrial action and unemployment. The north was particularly decimated. Apart from Kent and London in the dark for midweek darts, I had rarely left Hastings and certainly never stayed anywhere and lingered. So, when I say to you that my memories of that first jolly to Jollies were not the darts, you will piss your pants when I tell you that for the first time in my life I saw a Doner kebab shop.

These were unheard of in Hastings. No word of a lie, they did not exist. For a pound, I could feast on this new culinary delight and probably succumbing to the stereotype of what a darts player might be, I bloody loved it.

Once I started, I couldn't stop. We fell into a dirty repetitive cycle of darts, beer, nicking petrol, eating kebabs, sleeping in the car – and we were pretty pleased with ourselves. Hygiene was for later; hi fives were for now.

I recall very little of the darts! But clearly, it was the carrot. Unfortunately, our disgusting etiquette caught up with us. On the way home, I was farting for England. The smell was rancid. The guys had had enough and pulled over on the M6, man-handling me out of the car, throwing me in the boot for the rest of the journey. Let me tell you – Stoke to Hastings is 235 miles. That is a long way to go when you can't breathe, whether because you are in the front due to what was coming out of my behind or whether you are locked up behind because you had the front to pump for England.

Well, I settled down in the boot for the long ride home – not that such a concept exists, bumping along on the M6 in total darkness with an uninsured driver. As fate would inevitability have it, we made it all the way to the edge of Hastings when, from nowhere, the car pulls over. One of the lads in front bangs on the back seat and I thought that meant we were almost home.

Oh no, it didn't mean that at all.

Then, I could hear the engine being turned off...followed by muffled voices. I still assume we are home. Oh shit.

The boot opened. I felt like I was in one of those movies when the Nazi was putting the spotlight in the POW's face. Geez, we hadn't done anything wrong. Oh yeah, apart from the no license and syphoning petrol bit.

Oh – and the fact that the police officer standing over the boot staring at me recognised Paul from a previous traffic offence. So, none of us were legal and one of us had previous!

The clues were all there. A petrol can with two syphoning tubes and a body in the boot.

'You're nicked,' said the stereotypical sitcom copper.

And off we headed to the station. All that fucking way and now this – some jobsworth policeman pulling rank because he could. And because he was right!

A long journey looked like descending into a long night. The crimes ranging from kidnap to syphoning...

One by one we began to hope and wriggle free.

'Show us your license,' the cop asked.

Colin's license seemed to pass the test...

Dave, of course, had signed his name as Colin on the

31

paperwork from whom he had borrowed the credentials.

Kids – there was no photo ID then either.

This was agony – we were just 100 metres from home.

Then – relief.

'Everything seems in order,' the officer confirmed.

He had had his fun with us and we were free to go. Even though he should have detained us. You can add identity theft to the charge sheet.

Then Dave committed a schoolboy error.

'Can I use your loo?' he asked.

'The toilets are out the back through the office and I will have to accompany you,' said the cop.

Well, you never know who might just be pissing in a constabulary urinal, do you? Then Dave hears footsteps and the unzipping of flies…

'What are you doing here, Dave?' asked a mate of his from football…who happened to also be a cop on shift there.

'Dave?' said the first plod. 'I thought your name was Colin.'

Next thing: Nicked. Court. Fine. Points on the license. No license to put points on. It *was* all a bit like that classic *Great Escape* moment when the German officer speaks to the Brit at the station in English and he replies back, blowing his cover fleeing down the platform and getting a bullet load in the back. Just when you are smug enough to think you have made it, then comes the killer blow.

The humiliation was Dave's – or Colin's, if you like – but we all felt obliged to chip in for the fine. It was the right thing to do and he had to take one for the team. Kev and I handed over what we had. Paul and Dean drew a blank.

To this day, Dave still awaits the cash. And fuck knows who Colin is.

But, you know what? We had a great weekend and the comedy end to the story means it serves long in the memory and even though we clearly did wrong, we can laugh about it now and it makes that trip even more memorable.

The key though is that whilst the others were there for a laugh, I was in. My first time at a tournament. A proper tournament.

I saw them walk on stage and a glaze fell over my expression. I didn't crave attention of superficial fan worship but it was all part of the spell. All I wanted to do was shoot darts but now I could see how popular it could make you and how exciting it all was. When you were new to it – and on the outside of it – it just looked amazing.

Before a dart was thrown, I already had one conclusion.

This was what I was born to do.

Chapter Six

A Different League

In my head, I had gone through the gears. I knew definitely where I was heading. It was just a question of how quickly I could get there and if I could do so in a legitimate vehicle. I was now playing seriously…and playing seriously well.

I looked around me at my peers and started to glance upwards at whom I had to beat rather than down below at those whom I always wipe the floor with. First person on my radar was Rod Booker from Haywards Heath. We were both peaking at the same time. He was a bit special.

This did not go unnoticed. Suddenly, I was in the county team for Sussex. Out of the blue.

Of course, normally you are in the B team and then if you are good enough, you make the seniors. My mate Gary, as the Team Captain, announced the squads. I was straight in the A team together with Rod. Both of us were to make our debuts against Pembrokeshire. Not one of the classic sporting fixtures in the calendar!

This promotion had never happened before and I couldn't

believe it.

Rod was ahead of me…a fantastic player, so natural. I told him that I just needed it to sink in for a bit. I knew this was a bit of a closed shop and breaking into that system was something that might never happen but they did work off the local averages and I was in. I don't know if they thought they were taking a chance on me or if I was a certain pick but it didn't matter. I had made it and it was my place in the team to lose. And when you are going through the ranks being up against an Eric Bristow is not even on your radar. You define 'making it' as getting to that next stage. You view it as recognition. Little things become massive things – going straight into the A team was a million miles from the World Championships that I had just seen *but* you can only climb the ladder one rung at a time and right now, I felt I had just soared into the skies.

Then the reality of sport hit me. I lost my debut to a Welsh international called Gareth Picton whom I have never seen since. I was dropped straight into the B Team. Even at this level, that was the brutality of the game. Rod was firing nothing but golden darts, storming the averages in the Southern Counties section of the league and went automatically into the Unipart British Professional Championships *and* therefore on to the TV. I looked on with pride and not quite envy but wondered if that might be where I was heading. I hadn't made it at all or at least, would have to make it again. He deserved it so I was pleased but I probably needed this lesson early. I am sure too some people were delighted at my fall.

By the end of the season, I was back in the As. I definitely needed that jolt. It was a blessing to enable me to sharpen that mindset. I was no longer just shooting darts and having a few pints in a local with people I largely knew. A competitive element had arrived that was more than playing your Dad's mate. Something greater than a tin pot trophy was at stake – your very right to compete at a different level could be taken away at a moment's notice. I worked this out as it unfolded before me. I had one conclusion. I had to better myself. Again.

I made an odd call but the right one. Sussex, as a county did not have a lot of ambition. This was my home patch. You do always want to play for your local team, don't you? Halfway through the next season, I fell out with Sussex! I think this represents the growing size of my ambition – but not ego. I knew I was becoming a big fish in a small pond. For some people that would have been the summit of their aspirations. But I wanted to swim with the big fish all the time and Sussex were in a comfort zone where they would always do what they had always done and that always means you get the same results.

Disillusioned, I contacted the Kent County Team. At the time I was playing for Tonbridge Super League and it was one hour away. It seemed an obvious move. Sussex did have some great talent. As a group of young players we *were* like a band of brothers. Rod, Mark Davis, Andy Wyth, Jim Withers were decent arrowmen and Colin Whiley went on to represent England, but Sussex as a mentality did not travel. I don't know if it was down to family life, lack of ambition or being comfortable where they were but for me that led to insular thinking it was not a winner's mindset.

Of course, against that inflexibility came a rigid set of rules but these were changing. Historically, Kent could not accept outside players. Then they could. But guess what? The system could then accept you but the other players couldn't!

I was straight in the B team. Rank was pulled.

At my first Kent home game, an imposing 6 foot 4 character called Dave Nash came over to me.

I was quite taken aback. I knew things could get parochial and that's why I left Sussex but Nashy was simply nasty when nobody knew who I really was.

'So you're the seasider,' he began. 'You wanna fuck off back to Sussex.'

I took an instant dislike to him though years later we became very good friends. Perhaps you can see why. The big ego had spoken.

We were supposed to be on the same team yet when I took to the stage they were all urging me on as Wingnut – because of the size of my ears, one of which you recall doesn't work. It is one of the odd things in sport that even though it is a given you have to

37

play the opposition, sometimes you have to play the enemy within.

So I was that hated that I was bricking it, constantly asking myself why I had put myself in this position and of course then doubting my ability as they, in malice, questioned my character. You should not be rocking up to the oche worried about the darts in front of you because of the knives behind you.

Once you overcome that internal pressure and you start hitting good darts, then the game changes. It took the rest of the season to win them over and I only did that through performances.

In the end, I played for Kent for seven years!

Chapter Seven

The Crafty Cock

Kent were simply Premier League and Sussex were Division Three. There was no animosity from my hometown side. Again – an insight perhaps into their lack of edge. We rarely played them.

Most importantly, I was meeting better opposition regularly and even though your fate is in your own hands when you throw the darts to the degree that it doesn't really matter how good the opposition are if you are on fire, of course you are more likely to play better if the other team are good! You raise your game accordingly.

And my new team oozed class too. Once I was accepted, I became an adopted man of Kent, or a Kentish man – whatever the correct turn of phrase was. They had told me so many times but I still couldn't get it right.

After cracking them, I realised I was surrounded by great team spirit and a bundle of laughs. It simply made me better playing week in week out with soon to be England international Ian 'Chippy' Carpenter, Ian 'Crusty' Covill who went on to win the televised 'Cockney Classic' hosted by Eric Bristow and get this, Andy 'The Viking' Fordham could only get in the B team at the time. Our skipper was Micky Norris, himself a former winner of the *News of the World* championships.

Norris does not appear to have a nickname. Someone was taking the Mickey.

The result was my confidence went through the roof. Self-belief is everything in this game and you often only realise that as you are coming down the other side of the business when you are a bit older, and younger players are coming through and they whip you just like you used to do all those years ago. But now, with this talent around me both as opposition and in my team, I went to a next level I didn't even know existed. Between 1989 and 1993 I had recorded 29 straight wins on the trot. It still stands as a Kent record. I don't think I would not have achieved this if I had remained at Sussex.

I was about to fulfil a dream.

England came calling.

It helped massively that Sam Hawkins was our Chairman at Kent. In that not very organised world that darts was operating in at that point, he was also an England selector. My move to Kent raised both my game and my profile and whilst I had just been concentrating on my darts, I suppose it was obvious that if I was doing the business for Kent, then I would get a go for England.

You were still talking about a tin pot administration back then though. There were very few true pros. A small handful were making a living solely out of darts. Most of us had jobs. I thought it was extremely odd when Sam turned up out of the blue at a Kent Super League game.

'What the fuck is he doing here? I asked myself.

'Congrats, Shayne,' he confirmed. 'The board have met and you're in the next England squad.'

I was blown away but you can guess what happened next, can't you?

I shot the worst darts of my life that night averaging just seventeen. It was inevitable really. I don't know how that happens in sport that somehow I had either relaxed or my mind had wandered off to the future or if maybe 'making it' took that edge off me.

Sam had seen enough of me already though, patted me on the shoulder, and told me not to worry. I think my nerves were sky high despite the biggest vote of confidence you could ever get in being picked for your country. I was used to playing in a pub in front of ten people, maybe 25 at best if it was nine a side but now, I was going to play for England. Sport was very different in the 1980s whatever game you played but it is almost laughable that you could be transformed from this to the national team and be able to deal with it.

But this is what I had strived for. The step up only served to show just how amateur the game was. Of course, to play international sport, everyone has to make sacrifices and over the years I would abandon relationships, lose out on jobs that I still desperately needed to pay for life with, and I was always compromising my freedom because I was driving myself around still with no driving license. The rise to the national team didn't mean you were entering a pampered world of chauffeurs and top hotels and never having to go back to the day job. In fact, it just piled on the pressure on all those aspects of your life. This is where sport was in that era.

So, when you turned up for what should be the pinnacle of your career, you were always knackered, often had a row with the current missus, were driving late, fast and illegally and could barely afford the petrol to get there.

And that is the stupidity of sport and what ambition does to you. As I got better and better on that 29 game streak, I literally did dream of playing for England. That was pride and for knowing that I was at the top of my game. There was another motive too of course. I desperately hoped that I could somehow in the dark age of amateurism make a living from it. That was probably the real dream. To be able to stuff the sausage factory and all the other shitty jobs up their own backsides.

With hindsight, having to take that path perhaps kept me grounded. When you do a hobby for a living, what do you do for a hobby? I had no choice but to have two lives.

The game *was* changing slowly though and every rare time there was a televised match, you got drawn in. It split households.

You were either in one camp or the other, and for me, Mum and Dad that had always meant the wee Scot, Jocky Wilson.

Even though I later got to know Eric Bristow quite well, we didn't like him at the time. Nobody in our house thought he was a nice person – puffing arrogance every time we saw him. What I later came to realise was that he was the first celebrity of darts and he knew it. If I am honest, he defined superstar. Many people did hate him. Few knew him. He was friendly with a small circle and appeared rude to others. He was not just the crafty cockney. At times, he could be a crafty cock.

But, but, but...none of us would be here without him now. Pre-Eric, it had been a game played by stuffy old men in their cardigans in smoky pubs. It takes such a divisive figure to polarise opinion and bring the game to the masses and you simply can't overlook one thing. In front of a dart board, he had the skill to back it up. It is one thing to strut around like you own the place but the fall was immense if you couldn't support it with the arrows – and my, he could. In short, he set the bar at a new level for performance and for performing. That meant he emptied the bar.

His persona and his darts made him unbeatable unless you were John Lowe or Jocky really – and I think that is why we loved Jocky because when you are fan and you are inevitably blown away by the darts, any underdog that can knock the pantomime villain of his perch will suffice. Jocky was working

43

class, loved his beer and always had a smile on his face. He seemed to have the best shot at taking Eric down.

It is only when you start to have the opportunities yourself to appear at this level, without necessarily being on it, that you take a step back from how you saw it as a viewer. Again, just like moving to Kent, it gives you an edge. You start to think about who you will be as a darts player rather than just letting the darts do the talking. That is both a plus because you are becoming professional in your mind but also a distraction because you do not want to over-think it.

Eric was simply a pioneer. He was one of the first to have his name on the back of his shirt. Everybody followed. I wouldn't have even thought about anything like that. And when you have a shirt with your name on the back, you have to get that nickname on too. Nobody initially had a nickname or a shirt. Eric now had both – albeit through the unlikeliest of means. The Crafty Cockney comes from a pub in Los Angeles, of all places.

The pair were essentially years ahead of me in skill and image. In the years 1986 to 1992, all I did therefore was mile after mile and dart after dart. The goal: to better myself. The purpose: to put myself somewhere near the top of this mountain from which these two rightly could look down on all their peers.

Picked for England, and I could join them. Impose myself on the game and riches would follow. Or so I thought...

<u>Chapter Eight</u>

Three Lions on My Shirt,
One Chicken Dinner On My Plate

The British Darts Organisation (BDO) sent me a letter to say I had been 'picked'. How different were things back then!

England internationals used to be a massive televised event and very well attended in person. The matches were no longer shown and not many people were now turning up. That was the broader picture.

Enclosed with my note of selection was an expenses form and details about my uniform. I would soon be donning red flared trousers and a red and white Lycra England top – or as almost everybody called it at the time in acknowledgement of those colours, The McDonald's kit.

They needed to know my chest size though Heaven knows why. The top was like wearing a second skin in the way that it clung to you so tightly. Nor could you do up the trousers. They killed you in the crotch. I would look every inch a clown.

The letter explained that funds were tight so I couldn't go

mad on expenses. That is all very well but I would need a day off work for starters. This was international sport and I had to ask for leave! I could claim for petrol and a few incidentals too.

I thought I had better phone them. There was no way I was performing in this outfit. I could barely get in it. My mind was eased when they told me not to worry, they would sort me out when I got there. Of course, they would. They were an experienced organisation running darts and I was new to this. And this was international sport. They had done this hundreds of times before.

So, here we go. All roads led to The Lakeside Country Club at Frimley Green. My international career was about to start.

I drove myself there, slightly intimidated. I didn't really know any of the players though they knew of me. Phil Taylor, Dennis Priestley and Captain Bob Anderson were in. Eric was not. He had been dropped – amongst others at my expense – which in itself was just extraordinary. The legend of the game was no longer in the team. The man whom I had heckled from a sofa whilst I dreamt of his status was now behind me in the pecking order. It gives you confidence and takes it away. Wow – I am good enough to displace Eric. Wow – am I good enough to displace Eric? The highs and lows of sport...the tricks of the mind.

Before I could even begin to think about making my name, there was nothing but hurdles to jump through. On arrival, I made straight for the officials. It had been on my mind all the way up. Because of the nature of darts around this time, the honour and status of playing for England was severely watered down by process. I sensed it before I had even got there. I couldn't perform in that kit and I was going to be broke if they didn't cough up. There really was no time to dream.

They took me out the back – a phrase that in itself tells you just how amateur it was. There was no kit man, no official area. Anybody could wander in and help themselves and now it was my turn. It was like walking into a second hand shop. Inside a massive truck were about 50 pairs of second-hand trousers.

'Sort through that lot and find a pair that fits you,' I was told.

(The curious thing is that as time passed, trousers began to become a superstition. I hated adhering to the dress code. The more I conformed, the more I played shit. I preferred to play in my jeans but at some tournaments you couldn't so I probably hold the record for winning more money than anyone in other people's trousers.)

Playing for your country gave you no choice or flexibility. You were turning up for a Ronald McDonald audition.

By about the 20th search, I stumbled upon a pair that fit like a glove. I got lucky. They hadn't been washed, had Bobby George's name in the lining, the pockets were cut out and they were slightly soiled. International sport and its humblest beginnings.

Bobby was a bit of a legend too but he wasn't getting picked any more. We all had an eye on what he was doing. He looked like he was coining it in, doing a lot of brewery contracts and exhibitions. That was where the money was – *not* playing for your country.

Once I was kitted out – if you can call it that – I was sent over to another desk to sort out the expenses. I handed it to a lady behind the table who without looking just put it in a locker. In return, she gave me an envelope – the same envelope she gave to everybody.

I protested that I had had handed in over £120 worth of expenses. No response. I nearly died when I opened the envelope. Inside were £15 and a voucher for chicken and chips – once.

That was the fee for playing for England.

And yet, I am in no doubt that the BDO put my £120 expenses through their books. Why did they even bother sending me the form in the first place? Second hand trousers that I had to search for, and £15 for a chicken dinner. You were meant to puff out your chest and represent your country. Genuinely, I was deflated before I even played.

My debut came against Scotland. I was pitched against Alan Brown, a nice guy whom I had seen around at a few tournaments and now in a few chicken restaurants too! I beat him 3-1, which was a relief by this stage more so than excitement. You didn't want to fail or look out of place – however much the BDO did their best to do exactly that! I narrowly missed out on Man on the Match which Mike Gregory took by one dart from me. But it didn't matter. I was in. And not out of my depth.

I was non-plussed though by the whole experience. For the first time, I got to know a few of the players but bar a few Welsh in the crowd, the venue was sparsely filled and nothing like the atmosphere I had experienced in 1984. I thought it would be rip-roaring. Shortly after, I did appear on TV for the first time at the World Championships which was a good indicator that my profile was rising as they did not broadcast all the games. This, though, was almost a non-event.

It was clearly not the route to fame and fortune. TV coverage was then for insomniacs and the rewards just for playing were minimal. It was utterly ridiculous for anybody who worked who wanted to watch. And it wasn't much better for the players either. Something had to happen. By the time I was picked for England for the final time a decade later, I told Pauline Stafford from the BDO 'no more'.

She was to approach me at the Eastbourne Open to inform me that I had been selected. I asked her when the fixture was. The fact that I didn't even know is telling and an indicator as to how far away that would in time become as an ambition.

I had just hit my first competitive nine-darter and went on to achieve something which I do not believe anyone has ever done:

I hit *three* nine-darters: here, the Sussex Super League

Singles and in the Tonbridge Open.

I have also had two against me! One was in a head to head with Phil Taylor and another by Martin Phillips in the semi of the Isle of Mann Open. And I chalked one for Alan Warriner against Roland Sholten in the Irish Classic.

I have asked the oracle Facebook and drawn a blank. I believe this remains some sort of record.

Forgive me if my mind was therefore on other things at the invitation.

When she told me, I simply said I couldn't do it as I was playing at an exhibition in Jersey. Her response was that if I turned England down, I would never ever get picked again.

I had to break it to her that playing for my country wouldn't pay my mortgage but playing Jersey would. I acknowledge too that so many players reading this would willingly throw their grandmother under a bus to represent their country.

I simply replied that I had been there, worn the ill-fitting T-shirt and all I got was chicken and chips. By that stage and several years later my ambitions had changed of course – and so had the game.

In 1993, came The Split.

Chapter Nine

The Split

It had been brewing for at least a year.

A group of elite players including Phil Taylor, Eric, John Lowe and England colleague Dennis Priestley looked to form a breakaway movement. I was never contacted nor part of the discussion.

The British Darts Organisation and the newly formed World Darts Council were at loggerheads.

It was a pivotal moment in sport and broadcasting. The new Sky-backed Premier League had lifted English football out of the doldrums of European bans, racism, crowd trouble and several stadium disasters where only a couple of live matches were shown on TV every year to several games every week, and a huge influx of cash which meant some of the biggest names in football were all rocking up now in the new tournament. Wages escalated, profiles went through the roof. Analysis went into overdrive. Football was back. Other sports like cricket and rugby followed in time. Darts would never be in the same league but for its audience, its organisers, its sponsors and its broadcasters, there was a massive hole in the market. A select few spotted the opportunity.

At the heart of this and alongside that general feeling that everyone had been underpaid for years was what we all knew to be true. Darts was not run properly.

I refer you back to Exhibit A – the chicken dinner.

Earnings were on the slide towards a bare minimum. Eric and a few elite other pros had been doing OK based on their huge personalities and obvious ability, but the money was coming from the former not the latter. You simply had to rely on the odd tournament win here or there to survive and if you had a good agent like Eric, a chap called Dick Alex, then exhibition work would come your way. Only Eric and a handful of others were in that game.

But Dick Alex was no dick. Nor was his mate Tommy Cox. A Dick and Cox grabbed the game by the balls.

Together with John Markovic they changed the face of darts forever. They were almost a secret society. Nobody knew what was going on outside of their circle but overnight it just exploded and suddenly there was now a darts championship on Sky too.

It was so cloak and dagger that I can tell you that the day The Split was announced it was the first I had heard anything about it – ridiculous really, considering I am supposed to be an England international and perhaps therefore might be an asset to the package.

Of course, it is not called The Split for nothing. To this day, it is still referred to as that. Nobody talks of 'a new world' or 'the formation of a premier league'. It is The Split. That meant of course, there was a fall-out.

Born out of divisions and resentment, it created divisions and resentment.

As quickly as it happened, the BDO banned everyone involved instantly. They were persona non grata – ostracised and hung out to dry leaving uncertainty as to what this future was when the alternative was the shambles they had come from.

Nobody knew politically how it would affect their status. It was just obvious that darts needed TV and professional darts players, of which I only became one around 1994, needed a better financial structure for those involved.

Hindsight tells you that there was nothing to lose but the old traditional governing body of darts threw its toys out and played on that doubt that is laughable given the power and success that Sky now has.

The BDO made one simple calculation – if they banned you, you would come back.

Everyone was running scared. The new organisation needed, in effect, 32 players to make a tournament. If people weren't signing up straightaway, then they had nothing to show. It was a game of cat and mouse and nerve, and I certainly was unsure what to do. On the one hand, the Sky was the limit, on the other your brain was saying nervously to wait. Nobody could know that TV and sport was going to be such a hit at that particular moment. Again, looking back that fear and doubt is ridiculous. Of course, we know now how satellite TV has transformed even minority sports like netball.

Some people who weren't part of the original group signed up at the first 'new' World championships. Players like Graeme 'The Fish' Stoddart, Mick Manning, Kevin Burrows and Dennis Smith made the move over to the dark side. It really was a testing moment. I was getting more free chicken than I was pound notes at this point and still scraping by doing jobs for the council – in the England team but getting cash in hand work by putting business cards out there, tarmacking roads for the local authority.

In effect, darts was in disarray. The sport was immature in its business mindset. The concept of an international working for the council defied the mentality of what it should take to play for your country. Plus, the BDO and the *World* Darts Federation (WDF) were behaving like cry-babies and expecting universal approval at the threat of worldwide bans but the reality is that they didn't have the clout that they thought they did.

It really does represent a line in the sand – like Maggie taking on the unions, like Sky saying we will broadcast live football, like the Internet moving the goalposts of everything. Imposing worldwide bans was one thing but when Germany, Canada, USA, and the perennial neutrals told them to fuck off, the gloves were off and their bravado turned out to be bullshit – old school with no legal spine, desperately hanging on to another era.

The stupid thing is, I was *still* in the England team. But there weren't many of us left. Most had gone and the national squad consisted of virtually all new players. Fresh blood was on the scene and the national squad bore almost no resemblance to what had gone before. From the blind side, albeit a prolific tournament winner, Martin Adams – Wolfy – was suddenly the England Captain.

Yes, it was an honour to be given the job. The role itself meant nothing. You couldn't influence how people would throw the darts. But somebody had to be it. I actually recommended him. When he got the nod, I thought – well, he works hard and he is the tallest, so fair enough he can lead us and that was always good for the team photos! But darts was in disarray. He turned out to be the best captain England ever had. For him, a void had opened up and he walked straight into it.

You couldn't reasonably know every time you put on that ill-fitting shirt if it would be the last time you would do so. All the talk was about the breakaway and we reached a situation where playing for your country just wasn't a priority because the other option of just Finally concentrating on darts under the new regime was much more attractive for money and exposure.

So, little did I know that the Home Internationals in 1993

against Scotland, Northern Ireland, Wales and Republic of Ireland *would* be my last. This was to be the end of the road.

I think it underlines the sentimental worth plus the accumulation of dreams of playing for the national team, that I had never been more nervous at that tournament – even though I had one eye (and obviously only the one ear) on what was going on elsewhere and *that* was now definitely greater than playing for England.

Once the F.A. Cup was the biggest football match of the season. Today, in 2019 it is not. This was the scenario I was coming to terms with. England just was not *worth* it any more.

The whole time you are playing in a tournament with this going round in your head, you feel a bit of a fraud. You know at the end of the weekend players are going to look at you and think that you had something else on your mind – which I did. It doesn't stop you throwing the best darts you can but it takes that mental edge away so the best darts you can is not really at the same level as you have set for yourself.

So, in the final I am on last against Ken Thomas for Wales. It is 12:12 – best of 25.

One last time I am playing for England and it's sudden death. I am physically shaking. My back leg is wobbling. And I hadn't even had a beer. I needed more than one. I really struggled to stay in the zone talking myself through every shot saying 'hit that red bit.' I felt worse than any televised game I had done and TV always brought that extra edge. It is as though my body knew what my mind didn't.

Somehow, I signed off in style. Ken fluffed a bullseye leaving me to take out a Double 4. I finished the hero for the day.

And whatever you thought of the sixteen pros who had jumped ship, and even though they had already done better than most of us out of darts, it was their agents that led the revolution. In short, the BDO paid little and you got about the same back.

The knock-on effect was instant. Suddenly records and rankings were wiped and I had found myself soaring up to Number Four in the world. That looked good – if anyone was noticing. It felt less so because even though you always want to be top dog, you do really only want to get there by beating the Erics and John Lowes of this world.

In everybody's story there comes a light bulb moment. And that was the first Christmas after The Split. I don't know what Santa brought you that year but he brought me The Tripod.

And that was a former barman from Holland named Roland Scholten. There you go – fitting the stereotype – runs pub, plays darts! Roland was a very tall and with his particular throwing technique, he became very consistent. He was certainly unique.

Roland was staying at mine. We always went to the pub to practise. The WDC had their own World Darts Championships which were on Sky. The pub was showing all the games. I am not sure if the public really knew the full extent of what was evolving in front of them and the complexity that now lay at the heart of such a superficial working man's game. If they did they would have spotted a few obvious signs.

Roland and I got it straightway that the tournament was being bulked out mostly with Americans with little or no stage experience. They were good players but just didn't have the charisma, totally lacking in showmanship. Unusual for Americans, I know! There was razzmatazz, dry ice, walk-ons but no crowd. In truth, it was all a bit flat. Soulless. I thought it wouldn't last five minutes and I was better off sticking with what I knew.

It did have two plusses – cash, and viewers but I really doubted it would survive. For the time being, I would concentrate on being a big fish in a deserted pond. Now, I really did have a chance at being World Champion.

<u>Chapter Ten</u>

Hit The Road Jack

'I've got a proposition for you,' Dave Stevo Stevenson cornered me.

In time we would be inseparable mates. Now, he was just an acquaintance from the Kent leagues, whom if I am honest, I thought was a bit shifty.

'I've come into some money,' he continued. 'Shall we go round the world?'

It came right out of the blue.

'I will pay for everything; you'll go pairs with me and we will go 50:50 on the money.'

He was thinking the USA, Canada, Finland, Australia. I was thinking this could be the ticket to put money in the bank. I had no ties, and couldn't wait to get started. Saying goodbye to my then day job of tarmacking roads for the council was not going to break me!

'When do we go?' I asked him.

And before we knew it, we were off.

With a mate Barry Nelson in tow, we headed first for the Los

Angeles Open where I lost in the Last Eight to Dennis Priestley and then on to the Pacific Masters in Brisbane. This was more like it.

The night before the Brisbane tournament, there was a dinner-dance. We just sat there like outcasts in the booth. Then suddenly the music stopped and the spotlight turned on us.

'There's the fucking Pommie contingent. They think they're gonna nick our money this year.'

Well that was all we needed to spur us on.

I only went and won the thing beating two of Australia's finest – Russell Stewart in the semi and Wayne Weening on a tiebreak in the final. I did nick their fucking money. Not much of it, though.

My prize? £500 on a dodgy exchange rate and a plastic carriage clock! The chicken dinner was yesterday's news! It makes me laugh that you could go on the old TV show *Bullseye* and the public would win a speedboat. To this day, Mum still has it on her telly.

Just to clarify my clumsy language there. Mum does not have a speedboat on her TV, nor is she watching re-runs of Jim Bowen's show. She proudly displays my loot from Brisbane there! It meant that little to me as an ornament that I just said to her 'here are, have this' and she duly accepted. Wayne walked off with a crystal punch bowl. I am sure the Aussies switched the trophies.

We were bombing all over the place, back and forth across continents having a laugh and now not really part of the BDO versus WDC split, though I was still BDO and picking up ranking points. I was just a million miles from it.

The venues too were much more exotic than Essex.

We arrived at Laughlin, just outside Las Vegas – a gambling town hotter than Nevada's capital itself. We each paid around £130 each for a four-day jolly. Everything was included including transfers, accommodation, free food and beer. And 32 sweaty, pissed-up darts players. What a brilliant tournament.

We were all shitfaced. For days. After 20 or 30 White Russians, I am falling off my stool. I was due to play pairs with Andy Fordham the next morning against Cliff Lazarenko and Jocky Wilson but when I got up, I threw up spewing congealed milk and chunks of yoghurt everywhere. The place was a state and so was I. I know what you are thinking. Darts players don't eat yoghurts.

Even in the Singles final, where I lost to Rod Harrington, I was wasted. Stupid really – that you can't get arrested for chucking darts pissed in the name of sport.

We were all in the same boat. Of course, banter was king and the booze did the talking. I was practising when a gobby Eric sidled up to Stevo to deliver a few home truths.

'Hello, how you doing?' The Crafty Cockney began. 'I saw you in L.A. I thought I might see you in Vegas.'

Stevo explained that we had skipped Vegas and headed to Brisbane.

It sounded like he was building up to something.

'I hear you are sponsoring Shayne these days,' Eric began.

'Do you want a word of advice about sponsoring Shayne,' he offered without being asked. 'You should be backing Fordham. He is going places. Burgess is a fucking idiot.'

Wow – that was a bit strong.

'It's all taken on board, Eric.' Stevo replied.

'By the way who won the Pacific Masters?' Eric asked.

'That fucking idiot there!' Stevo replied, pointing at me.

For once, Eric was speechless.

Chapter Eleven

Hungry For More Than A Fucking Chicken Dinner

In 1994, Bobby George reached his second BDO World final, the first after The Split. There had been a long gap since the last one. He was probably the most recognisable figure left in the BDO.

My win at the Pacific Masters had qualified me – fucking idiot that Eric thought I was.

I turned up at The Lakeside Country Club thinking this had to be my moment. I wouldn't get rich but I might get the status. After all, about 80% of the field had never been on television – so low profile were they.

In the first round, I drew Meatloaf, or as his parents christened him, Steve McCollum. I knew him well as we had played together for Kent on several occasions and went on to be an England international. There he would stand with his big long curly hair and his great big puffy shirt.

I made the fatal mistake of thinking I would get him out of the way and then concentrate on the Second Round. There is a fine line between confidence and cockiness and often you will only see the latter in the players even though it is just for show.

That day, I had talked myself past Steve before I even threw a dart.

I am out losing in the first round. Steve absolutely bashes me. I think I only win one leg.

I make £350. And no chicken dinner.

Crucially, there had been no reaction financially from the BDO money wise. They were simply waiting for the sixteen or so players to come back from the PDC

It takes a moment like this to realise. I had hit rock bottom. I knew I had to re-build. I am getting knocked out early for not much cash in a tournament I thought I was going to win and everyone else I had been playing against for the last few years was swanning off onto satellite TV.

The stupid thing is – I was still in the England team. Pissed up abroad, nowhere to be seen at home and on the fringe of the breakaway darts mafia, the national selectors were still picking me.

Unfortunately *they* didn't get it and I was fast cottoning on. The truth was that playing for your country was not the pedestal you thought it would be. There has always been an argument in any sport that it should be an 'honour' and that you ought to be prepared to do it for free.

That was majorly missing the point. The TV carrot had been dangled. Many had cut and run. All each of us wanted was to play in tournaments and make a living out of the game. I knew that on my day, I could beat anyone. Playing for England was the least likely way to do so. If you had the chance to get 100 'caps' for England and therefore 100 small chicken dinners, or the opportunity to travel the world and make some serious cash that you could eat out in any chicken restaurant with you wanted then you would probably do the same. Nothing summed it more than the price and the concept of chicken.

A male chicken is called a cock. The existing business proposition to avoid going rogue was essentially being protected by male chickens.

I did head back to England and then on to Finland where I met and played pairs with Ronald Sholten, which we duly won only to then get demolished in the final of the Singles by some seventeen-year-old kid. It didn't matter that the lad deserved to win. If you are good enough, you are old enough. The accumulative effect though meant that I did not see the reality that I had come second in a tournament… which is always still a pretty good achievement. I just processed it that I had gone to Finland and some teenager fresh out of school had beaten me.

I don't know if I was going through the motions or if at the back of my mind I was thinking 'what the fuck am I doing, I really need to get on the other tour…' but you can see that every time something didn't go 100% right for you, you were leaning just that little bit more to crossing over. You were on a to and fro of self-doubt.

As fate would have it, decisions were sort of being made for me. The next stop for Stevo and I was Canada and the bizarre scenario that a tournament might have joint WDC and BDO ranking. By this point, I had got to know a few of those playing on the WDC circuit and of course all that did was fuel uncertainty and envy within me.

But in Canada, I got chatting with an old mate Graeme Stoddart who had joined the WDC just after The Split along with players like Dennis Smith, Mick Manning and Mark Thompson.

'I am absolutely loving it. You should join.'

He told me exactly what I needed to hear and probably already knew. I trusted him and was a better player so if he was happy, I surely would be.

'At all these televised tournaments, I am getting £800 to a grand just for turning up.'

That really was the clincher – *just* for turning up.

'I've no regrets. I can't get enough of it.'

Why so many before me – and most with lesser ability according to the rankings rather than in my mind – had shown no fear and just hopped over straightaway while I was still umming and ahing was proving to be one of the daftest pieces of thinking even a daft sod like me had ever had.

What was holding me back? My England place? Fear of being ostracised? The fact that I didn't even know anything about it before it happened and wasn't even asked an opinion? None of these were strong enough arguments to not go. Graeme was doing exactly what I had wanted – travelling and making a living whilst someone else picked up the tab.

In short, it took the comedy of a player called Kevin Spiolek to sum it up.

'Do you know what WDC stands for?' he asked.

'World Darts Council,' I obviously replied.

'Wads, dosh and cash,' he announced pissing himself laughing in the process.

Chapter Twelve

Three Words, One Future.

Jesus, if they were even giving it a nickname, then they knew they were on a busman's holiday. The fact that this was a clearly often repeated running joke told you they were rubbing their hands with glee and in effect taking the piss all the way to the bank. These guys weren't looking over their shoulder at all waiting for the BDO to show the full metal of a life ban. They had never had it so good.

If anything, their mockery of the initials just told you that they knew they had got their own back now. Years of trying to make it – late nights, smoky bars, low on fuel and funds to get you there...driving half-pissed on a chicken dinner wearing tasteless ill-fitting clothing – yeah, the BDO got exactly what it deserved and now they would take back from the game more than what it had taken from them.

I called a meeting with Alex and Tommy.

It was time.

'I'm thinking of joining,' I announced.

'We're always looking for decent players,' they didn't

exactly gush.

But I think I had a sense of my worth even though I couldn't really work out why they hadn't exactly come running to me.

'If I join will I be in the next televised tournament, and can I have two chicken dinners,' I negotiated.

Obviously, I didn't ask for the chicken.

'If you join this weekend,' they urged. 'you've got enough points to be in the Top 30 and you will be in the new tournament in July – the World Matchplay in Blackpool.'

With that, we shook hands, and I resigned by letter immediately from the BDO.

All roads now led to Blackpool.

I couldn't wait to get started to be honest. It was both a weight of my mind and a nervous wait to start. Far from thinking that I might have done a crazy thing and chucked in England and what we had all believed to be the traditional route into darts, making the decision cleared the mind and all I could see ahead were real possibilities.

I was going straight on TV and that's where the money was. Sponsorships and exhibitions that Eric had so coined in were now fair game for all of us – plus the basic was way up on anything I had ever known.

You can say you do these things for the money and the ego but quite simply, there was no alternative. Plus – the best players were there too and who wanted to be king of the BDO if you weren't testing yourself against meaningful opposition?

This proved true straightaway as I beat Bob Anderson in the Quarter Final. Bob, of course, had been my England captain and once I knocked him out I thought I was waltzing to victory in my debut tournament. You can never know though, and the need to get enough players in to build a proper tournament meant that the Yanks provided the unknown. Sure enough, in the semis, I lost to a guy called Larry Butler, who took everyone by surprise that week and went on to win the whole thing and to date remains the only American to win a UK televised tournament.

Significantly too, the whole shebang had come on a million miles from when we had watched it on the TV. The organisers had really got their shit together creating a proper electric atmosphere that still lives today. They had transformed the perception of darts overnight from what I saw growing up watching Jocky Wilson to what you now see many times a year.

And the tournaments were coming thick and fast – the Samsung Classic, the World GP, World Pairs. This was now serious business and properly marketed entertainment and for the player, it ticked all the boxes, and as we know there are only four of them… and none of them contain a chicken meal.

Cash, TV, on tour…and on the piss. This was the real deal.

And Graeme had partially mis-represented the fee. I was often getting a couple of grand just for going out in the first round, which obviously was not the intention. The money *still* could have been better for a TV event but my God, it was *much* better. Of course, it did not install any better standards in you. We still mostly spent it like it was going out of fashion – the idea of saving for a rainy day was non-existent. Every single day under the BDO had been a financial downpour. Now was the time to live and to make hay while the sun *was* shining.

I was coming to decisions fast. Stevo and I went our separate ways with him staying in the BDO. He should have come across of course, but it wasn't all an oversight on his part. He ended up managing Ted 'The Count' Hankey *and* Andy 'The Viking' Fordham, which in that era, was about as good as it can get. We know what Andy achieved and Ted won the World Championships twice – so no need for a hanky.

For me, the WDC journey was underway. Wads, dosh and cash. And America. I began to spend a lot of time in the States and those countries which were neutral to The Split and refusing to adhere to BDO rulings. We went where we could and when we could, on the road almost every other month. We did have to pay our own way and that meant we travelled as a group living in each other's pockets and splitting winnings fairly evenly so we all made all of the time. In essence, could there have been a more corrupt and less psychologically challenging model in sport?

This was supposed to be competitive and largely about the money. Any professional athlete wants to develop an edge over their opponent and here we were all clubbing in, getting the cheapest flights and accommodation and sharing up the cash. Athletes we were not clearly – pissheads, yes. The game was moving on but still not quite as professional as it should be.

Amidst the talk of cash and TV, it is easy to lose sight of the fact that you still needed to shoot some darts. It is all very well thinking you get a grand just for turning up but sooner or later if that was all you did then you wouldn't be asked any more. Thankfully, I wasn't in that position yet. In fact, I was close to the top of my game, losing one final in Chicago to Canadian John 'Darth Maple' Part and won all three men's titles in Boston. The force was with me! On that weekend, I pocketed £7500 alone – or approximately 750 chicken dinners.

I think you can get a size of how the razzmatazz was coming though by the fact that we were always in Vegas – a man-made city with a forever transient population of tourists, wanting immediate superficial entertainment on tap at all hours of the day. People were there for a good time not a long time – and darts seemed to fit that bill.

It didn't matter if you were there several times a year. Nobody would see you twice. You were, in effect, a show, just like the singers who do residency there. That probably takes some edge off the darts – the money remained but performance and showmanship started to take over – plus, of course, the booze.

In the heat and around the excess, there was nothing else to do nor any lasting relationships to be formed except with the

72

same faces on the circuit and it was here therefore that I got to know Phil 'The Power' Taylor – but only because I annoyed the hell out of him.

We were playing pairs in the American Cricket – Bob Anderson and myself versus Phil and Richie Gardener. The score is two legs all. Phil miscounts the last throw and thinks they have it.

He needed a single bull on his last dart.

He had shot Treble 20.

Bob is on his game and tells me 'he's mis-counted, step in.'

Bull. Double bull.

I clench my fist and punch it sky high.

Phil. Not happy.

'You, don't fucking large it in front of me.'

Me. Happy.

'You wanna learn to count.'

He left with the hump, embarrassed but for sure, we would meet again. As thick as us darts players are, most of us *can* do the maths. It is extraordinary that the majority of us do not possess many qualifications or brain cells but if only school had found a way to apply every sum to a dartboard, we would probably all be at Oxford by now.

In the Fox and Hounds, of course!

The fact of the matter is that we had all been living off crumbs. Phil was winning everything in sight. His irritation was probably part of the route to perfection. I just enjoyed the moment because these points were few and far between.

But, despite our omni-presence in the States, none of our matches were shown on American TV. Darts had been big on the box there in the late 70s and 80s but had receded in its popularity. If we could have somehow rekindled that magic, then who knows how big the game could have been. The Brits were providing the majority of the talent. Some Dutch stars like Raymond Van Barneveld were starting to emerge and obviously the Yanks and Canadians filled some of the early tournaments up post-split but with TV king and exposure everything, we still could not capture the imagination of broadcasters over the pond.

We had made a start though and repercussions of The Split were being felt at every level to such a degree that court was deemed the only option. Only in 1997, some five years later did a semi-resolution arrive in the Tomlin Order. Five years of shit that the early defectors endured in the background concluded when the BDO recognised the WDC and the right of players to choose which organisation to play for. In effect, anything else would be a restraint of trade – against the law. In return, the WDC acknowledged the World Darts Federation as the governing body of world darts and the BDO as the governing body of UK darts and renamed itself the PDC, Professional Darts Corporation.

So, in other words, what we all wanted – except we had long since past caring. We were on TV, we were on the piss and we literally on the money. A group of suits and lawyers who couldn't hit a bullseye in a million years, had taken five of posturing to decide fuck all without either really giving an inch.

We just kept taking the cash and shooting the darts. WDC. Wads. Dosh. Cash. PDC. Providers of dinners of chicken.

Chapter Thirteen

One Man Has The Power

Of course, whilst it looked like we were having the time of our lives, nothing is plain sailing and that period just post The Split was really uncertain. Darts players weren't really ones for thinking things through but they did have the nous – especially Eric – to understand a fair bit about image and their worth, and the whole Sky thing just made everyone wake up.

Before I made my mind up, mindful that the BDO were treating 'defectors' like lepers, Graeme Stoddart and I had that conversation at the Canadian Open when I had opened up that I was thinking about it.

I had been allowed to play. It was one of those tournaments where the Canadians didn't give a toss about The Split and a worldwide ban was something they were not going to get involved in.

Timing was everything. Stodd told me that I would love it and that there were loads of tournaments and that they were 'one big family'.

Literally as he spoke these words, glasses were flying

everywhere and a fight erupted. Phil Taylor grabbed the 1983 World Champ Keith Deller by the throat and carnage ensued.

'One big family?' I turned to Graeme for confirmation. 'Are you sure?'

Phil was in a rage. The Power had a short fuse.

'I had always hated you.' I heard him say to Peter 'The Fen Tiger' Evison.

They were clearly not a family and certainly not a happy one. I am standing there thinking only one thing – why would I join the WDC? Phil wants to beat everyone up. Sixteen pros thought they were superstars. Phil was sorting out the pecking order.

I had yet to play Phil competitively one on one. As you can see he had an awe about him – in front of the board and in amongst his peers. The first time we met for real was at the inaugural World Grand Prix at the Casino Rooms in Rochester, Kent. It was my first televised final after beating Peter Manley in a great tussle on a deciding leg of the semi. Phil already had a few world titles under his belt.

This was our first clash on an even keel. Such was his spectre, his reputation, his mental superiority that I was pacing up and down the night before. I couldn't sleep. Now, if you think about that, it shows he was the first player I had faced who cast that spell. At the end of the day, you threw the darts and if you hit the target, you win. It does not matter what your opponent does if you are on fire. But his reputation preceded him. He entered your mind before you entered the venue.

Plus – I knew we were live on telly at 7 pm. We had got accustomed to the bright lights but rounds of darts covered by TV were something you had not been used to. It was exciting but a conveyor belt. A final was different and you knew that not only did it stand out for the watching public and the live audience but your fellow pros were taking note too. It *was* a massive deal. I struggled to deal with the expectation and the pressure – and that is sport in a nutshell. Why should something you have done for years at a high standard be suddenly any different because it is on the box and has 'Final' next to it?

He had got to me. I was pacing like a lion – six hours before the match. This was not me. I decide to practise and make my way to the casino rooms. I keep telling myself I am going to be ready, I am going to be ready. But this was not how I prepared. You think of all those Vegas nights when I have been half cut and still delivered. Now I am finding myself walking up to the big glass doors of the main foyer to find a woman hoovering a carpet. I have to ask to go in and the cleaner waves me away, mouthing to come back later.

I am almost desperate. I bang on the glass where there is a poster billing the match.

'That's me…in the final,' I plead with her, holding my darts up. 'That's me in the final. I only want to go upstairs to practise.'

She relents for a second. Then out come the big keys.

She opens the doors and nods me on my way telling me that I presumably know where I am going. I walk into the back room.

My eyes deceive me. No, they don't. Phil is already there.

'Hey up ducks,' he mocks. 'Come for a bit of practise?'

I am beaten before we even start.

Sport *is* played in the mind. You have no reason to step outside your own to prepare for a game of darts. Now, mine was on loan to Phil and the whole business of paranoid second-guessing began when really it is a sport for one individual man blocking everything out with single focus.

'Come on then,' he chirped. ' Let's play beat the score...a pound a game. First to ten.'

We were the only two people in there apart from his driver. I should not have got sucked in. He was dismantling me bare. You can tell his confidence was supreme. He knew he had one up on me by the fact that he had arrived to practise before I did, leaving me of course questioning how bloody long he had been there. I guess he knew I would come and all that mattered in the game of the mind was that when I walked in, I saw him shooting for fun in a relentless rhythm, which wouldn't allow me to even get any going. Plus, look at the status of the man. The cleaner had locked him in as if nobody was to enter. I had to identify myself through a poster and practically knock down the entrance.

Then Phil's driver piped up.

'Wanna drink Shayne?'

'It's a bit early,' I replied without eyeballing him.

'It's never too early,' he came back at me.

That's why Phil had a driver!

'Phil likes a port and brandy.'

And I walked straight into it. Sucker punch.

After about half an hour, the same thing happened.

'Another port and brandy?'

'Nah, you're alright,' I offered unconvincingly.

Then proceeded to knock back another three or four. We drifted into the bar and Phil has already taken about £15 off me.

'I'll get these,' I thought I had better offer.

'If you insist,' Phil smiled.

They were just putting the float in the tills – and then it dawned on me.

'We're not open yet,' said the woman behind the bar. I am buying Phil a drink, he has fleeced me for £15 and the whole time has been helping himself to drinks. It was a put up job from start to finish.

Then we had to go on TV and he took me to the cleaners, wiping the floor with me 6:1.

I promised myself that I would never fold over again.

That's what I vowed. Vows don't last for long in the marriage of darts.

Chapter Fourteen

If The Shirt Fits

When the Tomlin Order came in during 1997, five years had been lost to bitterness, paranoia and disparity. Let alone, what the true records of the sport actually stood for. Who was world champion? Where were my ranking points? Where had all the money gone?

The truth is that all the bans were lifted and a lot of issues were resolved. Between 30 and 40 players defected in the beginning. Then, the figure ran into hundreds. It was a good club to be in. But, so much money went to lawyers. Think about it – players break away so they can Finally achieve a regular and decent standard of living. Two organisations battling it out blow much of that income on legal fees.

Even though the players really got on with it and it paved the way for the next generation to profit, it did leave its mark. Slipping out of that top tier damaged you psychologically – coupled with years of questioning as to whether the BDO bans actually were enforceable. When you came out of it all, you shook your head and wondered what it was all about. One of the more generous write-ups that I can assign to this time is that it does at least give you some context when otherwise your life was just a stream of car journeys and flights, Ports and Brandys and one bullseye after another.

And when *I* came out of it, I had a lot of time to reflect.

I had almost come full circle. I am in my first PDC World Championships. I am laying kerbs on Preston Road in Brighton for Sussex County Council. At the height and in the heat of mid-summer, I make my way in a high-viz vest and boots as dirty as hell to an Indian sweat shop with a sign outside saying 'all embroidery'.

I needed a snazzy shirt.

I was conscious of the fact that with the floodgates opening, there was a chance that I might appear on the box quite regularly. I could not run the risk, in a sport that was starting to get its act together and sell image, of turning up looking like I was playing for England! As daft as that sounds, that was the lowest point in my career in terms of how I presented myself.

If am I going on the box, I needed to ramp this thing up.

'What are you wanting, Sir?' a broad gesticulating Indian accent beamed.

'I'm a darts player,' I threw him a wildcard. 'And I am looking for a snazzy shirt for the television.'

'We are loving darts,' he replied. 'I am watching darts all the time.'

I am sure that he said equivalents to all his potential clients.

Equally, I don't think that he had ever had a darts player in there before.

'I'd like a shirt with Bulldog Burgess on the back in big gold type letters. How long will it take?'

He told me that I would have to wait three weeks – but of course, I would be having the finest darts shirt in all of the land.

Four weeks later, I am due on TV and there is no sign of any shirt.

A young Indian lad rings me.

'My Uncle has heart attack. He is making you the finest shirt in all the land.'

Even the kid was trotting out the lines now.

'It is not quite finished. Don't worry. I will finish the shirt for you. It will be ready next week.'

I knew they were giving me the run around. Nothing left to it – I decided to go round to the shop again in all my kerb-laying gear.

There was my shirt hanging in the window.

'Can I help you, Sir?' they asked as though they had never met me before in their life.

'I've come for my shirt,' I answered pointing to the window.

The young lad *has* never met me before.

'Oh no, Sir,' came the reply. 'That shirt is reserved for the finest darts player in all of the land.'

I was the finest player in all the land – according to his uncle.

And it *was* my shirt. Then he looked me up and down dismissively as I was still in my work kit.

'How will you be playing darts with all those big boots on?' he asked.

They did have a point. The rank amateurism of the sport meant that in the day job, apart from my weight, there was no way in the world I looked anything like a darts player, and certainly not 'the finest player in all of the land.'

Then again, this did not turn out to be the finest darts shirt for the finest darts player in the all of the land. The last two bloody letters that the lad had finished off were wonky.

I wore it once. And never again.

Chapter Fifteen

Top Of The World...

I became World Number One.

Unofficially.

For four days.

I had just lost in the final in Montreal to Darth Maple. Keith Deller, who was Head of the Rankings Committee took me to one side and broke the news.

'You've provisionally gone to Number One,' he advised.

I was over the moon.

'All you have to do is make the Last Sixteen in Saskatoon.'

That would ensure I would stay at the top of the rankings for about six months. For that, I would get a crystal glass decanter. Mum would need a bigger TV.

Except Phil had other ideas. Star wars were under way. Phil was always number one. His empire was about to strike back. He sent me crashing out at the Last 32. It was the worst possible time to play him. My reign lasted as long as the gap between the two tournaments and therefore didn't really happen. On such margins is sport defined. I slipped back to Number Three when in fact the way he demolished me made me look like a great big number two.

My best years were undoubtedly between 1997 and 2000 – for a couple of years in that period, I was on fire. On and off! You went up and down the rankings all the time but generally I was playing sublime darts and getting really good results. I was also fearless and I felt that made me mentally strong. Time would show that this was not actually strength but *confidence* created by form. Mental strength is something that you reach for in darker times. I was just playing well and that created focus. It did not however provide a platform for you to deal with more difficult times. But when you are flying, you don't over think it do you? All I knew was that I was consistently beating everyone except Phil Taylor bar one occasion in the Eastbourne Open but still wasn't really making big dosh.

It took some time for the post-Split mess to clear itself up. For the first ten years the PDC ran a points system and we all know what points make…prizes. In theory. I had had more chicken dinners than actual prizes I could convert. This meant that you might get ten points for a win, eight for a second etc but the system changed to a rolling two-year count based on how much money you earned and I afraid there was no place for chicken dinners in that league table. So initially, I was a shoe-in for staying in the Top 30 but only initially.

I had also moved to Walton on Thames in Surrey back in my

prime. This was mostly because of a woman! That meant I had been looking for new tournaments to keep ticking over and every Friday I would pay £2 to play in a tournament called The Meat at Walton Working Men's Club. I hate to say it but the prize was half a dozen sausages…and a chicken.

But I was struggling with it. Why was I playing? I was Number Three in the world but I had no contract or exhibition work. The maths really did not add up. Of course, as I would learn many times in the future, you still had to play really well to win regardless of who you were and I didn't win every week. As decent as the competition was, you knew you were lowering yourself even though you had regularly played equivalent Friday nights when you were making your way up.

It just did not seem right. World Number Three. (Former World Number One!) No agent. Big in Walton on Thames. Sometimes.

I tried to get my business head on. You cross a line at some point where you see lesser players doing better than you financially and the really good players – or Phil – coining it in and you wonder why when you are shooting such great arrows that you are not doing better. It wasn't jealousy. It just was something you couldn't understand. Plus, you also want to focus on the darts and not the sums.

I did attract one interesting sponsor who put about 7K my way. Mark Gardener from Hastings was one of the early big

Lottery winners taking home with his mate around £22 million. His business was Croft Glass but he was not a bad player himself so probably as a part vanity project but also because he had nothing to lose – he came on board commercially with me. I had hired an agent called Terry Avan who tried his hardest to get me where the others were but he had just a few contacts and couldn't make it happen. My relationship with Avan was brief. Though, as you will see soon my relationship with a van was to be long and lasting.

The situation was so ridiculous that the World Number Three actually asked Mark Gardener for a job. I had been struggling to make ends meet, despite being that high up in the rankings and I needed something to do in the week. I knew that his factory-made double-glazing and windows so I rung him looking for work.

He very kindly took me on. He invented a job for me.

They needed someone to sweep the floor.

I kept asking myself what the fuck I was doing. My business acumen was zero. I am World Number Three. I sweep the floor.

Mark Gardener also sponsored another Hastings player, the late John Russell whom I knew he thought was a better player but was also a very good friend of mine. I sensed that he was almost playing us as we played each other to see who might be the better option commercially going forward. You can imagine therefore that when Eric, Richie Gardener and myself went to do the draw for the World Matchplay live on Sky and I drew John in the first round that Mark was absolutely licking his lips at the dream tie!

I was shitting a brick thinking that in effect I was playing for more than a second round place or the kudos of a title. I was playing for my seven grand. Whoever lost this would probably place question marks in Mark's mind. But I shouldn't have even been in this position that I am entering a tournament against a mate whom I wouldn't want to come unstuck anyway but with no real commercial opportunities other than this one which was now on a knife edge.

Mark Gardener couldn't lose and thankfully I didn't! In a close game, I nicked it at the end and in time, John drifted out of the sport but it could have gone either way. The fact remains that to make my money, despite my ranking, I was calling in favours from a man who had money to burn. I am grateful of course, but you get the point that he was local, loaded and into darts. I hadn't really tested the commercial market at all. At the height of my success, nobody was doing worse! I kept thinking the money was coming – that I was making headway and my ranking would soon pay dividends. Tomorrow never comes!

But I was at least testing myself professionally. You will get the sense in this book that I am not interested in just listing tournament after tournament. Who wants to read a shopping list of stats? But some venues and competitions do stand out as markers to where your game was at.

To that end, the Yorkshire Classic at the Filey Bay Caravan

Park (!) was one of the hardest to win. I will tell you something else – no other sport in the world throws up venues like darts, does it!

My gut feeling was that there was a massive geographical influence in darts. Certain counties, like Kent, had better structure. Other areas like North Yorkshire, Northumberland and the North East just bred little superstars. They all seemed to be able to play. I don't know if it is simply fitting the stereotype of a working man's game and Dad went down the pits and Friday night was darts night but I always encountered a stiff level of competition and surprise packages. A lot of people could play so if 600 people turned up at Filey, you would reckon on about 400 having a chance. If you won anything in the North East, you had undoubtedly played some really good darts but also a universal certainty about sport rings true here. If you play a tougher field, you will probably raise your game. Towards the end of your career, when you are slipping and playing lower leagues again, that edge is gone and so lesser players can take you.

But, in 1998 when I won Filey, I was on autopilot – not going through the motions, but on absolute fire. I blitzed everyone. It left a reminder too that in amongst the outwardly superficial appearance of darts, there were issues and complications.

On the way to victory, I turned over the Middlesbrough-born Tony Eccles in the Quarter Finals. Eccles was The Viper which became highly ironic many years later as it emerged that he was actually a poisonous snake himself – imprisoned in 2014 for 16 years for rape and indecent assault on a young girl.

If ever there were proof in life that you just don't know whose hand you are shaking at the end of a tournament then this is it. I was actually using his darts until recently and had been for five or six years. He had lent me a set in Belgium on one of our trips and I had become very attached to them. Sports people do have their favourites and their superstitions.

Odd, I know.

Which is a much shorter sentence than Tony received from the judge.

I beat Darryl 'The Dazzler' Fitton in the Semi and 'Rocket' Ronnie Baxter in the final with a ten-dart last leg to win and to this day consider it one of my best victories. The prize was £1000 but oddly, I don't seem to have a trophy in my collection to commemorate what was a peak in my career. Much of the silverware was so cheap and tacky anyway that I have a feeling I lobbed the souvenir of one of my best performances into a field at the back of the caravan park!

The money was handy but the prize was no more than chicken feed. Ironic really, given that this was once almost my entire fee.

Chapter Sixteen

Camping It Up

I spent my life on the road. It made sense to live on it. By the summer of 1995, I bought a campervan. There was really only one reason I did this. Because Phil had one! It is only now as I read this as I really see the spell he cast on me and every other player in his era. Never mind the Port and Brandy, he was dictating where and how I lived.

But actually, it was bigger than that. He was setting new standards on the board, in his preparation and psychological warfare but also now how he spent life on the road, which – let's face it – was no life and was always… on the road.

We would rock up at a hotel and live by their rules – no superstar treatment as we were not superstars. That meant checking out when everyone else checked out and it meant the unpredictability of the times you would need a room when the tournament kicked you out.

Then we soon cottoned on. This was how Phil was saving money. He would park up near the big TV trucks and could come and go as he pleased. Another town, another tournament, another hotel for us. But Phil just drove a little further down the road with all his home comforts with him. He was sleeping in his own bed, cooking his own food, not kicking his heels paying extortionate prices in another faceless home for the weekend.

I really thought that of all the weapons in his locker, this was the smartest. More to the point from a personal lifestyle point of view, I really liked the idea. It suited me down to the ground. I wasn't a great socialite and I totally got the concept that you could feel at home miles from it and that would lift your whole game and demeanour.

I got myself a campervan.

Once Phil had one, of course the whole circuit was threatening to. None of us obviously had the funds that Phil did but economically, as long as we weren't constantly chucking money away doing repairs, it had to be a better deal than forking out for hotels and all those extras.

I could actually cook my own chicken dinner in the van! And it was a van – a scabby little transit that I converted to include a shower and a toilet. Its wheel arches were rusty as fuck but it never let me down. I wasn't allowed to park round the back in the car park with all the vehicles of course because I wasn't Phil and I lowered the tone so I just would find an old layby like a sad old man and that would do for the night. It didn't bother me in the slightest. I began to save a relative fortune and I know that even though the other players were gossiping about it, and I might have looked a poor man's Phil, deep down they wanted to do the same.

I could see possibilities ahead too. It could get me to Ireland and into tournaments in mainland Europe. I just bought myself a little bit of freedom and for the next seven years, this is how I lived.

It had an instant impact. If you lost, you didn't feel so bad about it because you weren't hanging around in a hotel. You were just able to cut off immediately or get the hell out of there. And let's face it, you did lose more often than you won, especially with how dominant Phil was. That was the nature of the beast.

I find a new friend in Mick O'Donaghue who tells me that I am doing six weeks in Ireland. Exhibition work. We get on like a house on fire and he has a lot of contacts in Ireland. This was just what I had envied when I saw Eric as I started out on the circuit.

I was in the form of my life, full of beans and with cash in my pocket. This could only end badly!

Obviously, I couldn't do all this on my own, and even though The Split still had some rank amateurism about it – like the travel arrangements - we all were getting wise to being professional.

It wasn't just the deal though – Mick got smart about the image. He could see the influence of television and worked out that if you were in the business of selling you needed a product.

Mick has his head screwed on. He was a good boy but a cowboy.

He was supposed to be coming with me all the way on the

94

tour and exhibition work on its own can be very dodgy. You put on a show, you have to let someone else ultimately be the star of it and you have to take all the banter from a breath away. You needed that wall of protection around you to just deal with all the elements of the night but Mick had to go back home for a few days. The simple equation is this. They all want a piece of you. You have to be Mr Nice guy for four to five hours. Everyone is trying to bend your earhole and you think 'it's only darts, they can have a pop'. All you have to do is smile and shoot one memorable game or just one dart and that is all people remember.

I missed Mick therefore when he wasn't there. He always had a cracking idea and a sense of venue and local mood.

One night we rolled into County Kerry and a pub in Tralee. Gaelic football was king – sod the darts. Kerry were up against Galway in the final. This was huge rivalry. Mick tapped into this immediately and decided to find a sports shop to get me a local football top with a hastily made Burgess on the back. The store loved it so much they gave it to us for nothing. For the best darts player in all of the land, obviously.

Mick wasn't just the king of the concept though. He got the drama and stage presence.

'Practise in your coat,' he told me. 'Then, go on in your coat. Do not take it off until I give you the nod.'

I had sixteen blokes to play. Nobody was saying a word. This was a traditional spit and sawdust pub where bodies were packed in and I am already getting incoming fire with people shouting 'get your coat off, you bloody English shit'. Some were threatening to walk out.

Then the moment came. Mick gave me the nod. Off came the coat. The crowd were gone. Not gone gone...gone wild. The jukebox hit the max, free beer was flowing and they ripped the floor up dancing. Never mind about the bloody darts. I could do anything after that. Mick had nailed it again. I don't even remember the rest but I am pretty sure you get the idea that there was no closing time and nobody had any idea what had gone on.

This is how myths and legends of great nights out began! Without Mick, therefore, I felt a little rudderless. My darts could speak for themselves and I could hold my own with the banter but you always felt a little pathetic walking into a venue and doing all the niceties yourself. It wasn't very showbiz to introduce yourself, as naff as that sounds. Plus, without that extra dimension that Mick brought, it just took some out of the fun from it too.

Next stop – a place called Listowel, home to a big Irish racetrack. A booker called Joe Flynn had organised two exhibitions, one in the middle of nowhere and the other in town. Ten of us clambered into an old minibus. This literally was the clapped-out vehicle on the road to nowhere. The roads were terrible and every inch of the way was single track. The cash and the beer aside – this was not what we got into darts for! In fact, as the minibus left the road and went three foot up in the air, I can honestly say that I have never been so scared in all my life.

I wasn't alone.

'Who is this driver? He is gonna kill us.' We all were saying the same.

He was on a death wish.

I suspect that he had done this route many times and in the same style.

Imagine our relief and disbelief when we Finally arrived at the venue to be told he was the local fucking serial arsonist who had torched barns and houses in the vicinity. The story goes that they were going to lock him up but instead...gave him a minibus license. We were close to tears when we get out.

It didn't get much better. Getting into the venue was a nightmare – pissing down and in howling wind and gales whistling at us at 80 mph, we had no choice but to be in for the night and that meant we were at the mercy of the locals. With the dartboard right in line with an open window, this was no night to play absolute shite. The darts were going in sideways! All over the place. I was playing rubbish but somehow good enough to win.

Conditions were that poor, I had to ask the landlord to shut the windows. He said he was obliged to leave them open because we were still in a smoking era and you would suffocate to death otherwise. I really was not playing well.

'You're just making fucking excuses,' the shy retiring Irish crowd whispered politely. Did they bollocks. They roared it out right under my nose then drowned themselves out laughing.

My guess? They had seen this weather before. They knew the local driver well and that's why he was sent. 'What the fuck am I doing here?' was probably the most repeated phrase on the circuit.

In for the night meant literally playing everyone. So, I did. As shite as I was performing, there are levels of shite and I was still good enough to win all my games. Finally, when I sat down, I knew that I still hadn't won them over!

'You're fucking shit Burgess,' one of them or possibly some of them piped up.

I gave them my most spontaneous witty reply.

'I know,' I mumbled.

And I had been.

Then the banter really started.

'I didn't hit 180 all night,' I protested.

As I said there are levels of shiteness.

'We shouldn't pay you,' the local venue owner interjected – and he fucking meant it.

And what could you do in a field of drunken Irishman with no escape and only an arsonist to drive you out of there? If he didn't want to pay you, you were not in a position to argue. Plus, I actually thought it was fair enough. I wouldn't have paid me.

But I wasn't done yet, and I knew the weather had a lot to do with it. So, I fought back.

'Shut the fucking window and I will show you,' I roared with a smile on my face.

I had no real idea of what I was going to do next but I had one or two exhibition shots up my sleeve.

'Get someone to stand in front of the dart board,' I heckled.

The John Virgo in me was getting ready to play.

'Name me a double,' I said.

I am sure he was thinking I was about to take him out.

'Fourteen,' he taunted.

So, I get this guy with a fag in his mouth to stand on a beer crate in front of Double Fourteen.

The first dart I throw goes through the tab and takes it into Double Fourteen.

The bar erupts.

'I would have done that all night if you had shut the fucking windows,' I bellowed.

And all they cheered. One dart and suddenly they thought I was king, and that was again all it took to be a hero. One memorable moment and you were high-fiving, drinking and dancing as though you were at a big family wedding. It was mad and fickle how you could work an audience and they could turn on you a moment. Suddenly, I was worth my fee.

This was a crazy place. I signed the fag. My cigarette is still in the pub there…in a glass case behind the bar! By midnight it was all over – except of course, it was just beginning. It is time for a long overdue piss. Then – well, I have never seen anything like it. I am standing at the urinal when I hear are the words 'girl coming in'. What the fuck.

A young lady was climbing in to the Gents toilets through the window. This was standard fare apparently. And I am not sure she was a lady. The Garda let you keep drinking but you have to lock the doors in these parts. Blind eyes turned. You are fine if you come in through the window. The local knowledge having a piss next to me helped her down and filled me in.

Half an hour later, there is a bang at the door.

'Put your pint down,' I was ordered.

It is now 1:30 in the morning.

The Garda walk in slowly and to silence.

Then they walk back out.

The music returns at full blast.

'What the fuck is all that about?' I ask.

I had seen some lock-ins in my time but that was just nonsense role-playing. When they weren't in uniform, probably those guys would have been standing next to me watching the same drill.

'If you had had a pint in your hand, they would have nicked you,' I was informed. 'If you put it down, they say nothing.'

It was like something out of the Middle Ages.

Then it gets worse…

The lady opposite me who is quite attractive regardless of the time and alcohol intake, bursts into song. She is a decent singer too. It is a perfect end to a crazy night. Starting to unwind after all the chaos that began with an arsonist and ended with the cops, I let myself go and start tapping away.

Then I look around and realise that all eyes are on me and those glares are uneasy ones again. After a few minutes it all stops. Somebody approaches her, whispers in her ear and she leaves.

'Sorry that won't happen again,' a complete stranger cum my new best mate apologises.

'What the hell was the problem?' Naïve old me asked. 'I was quite enjoying that.'

She had been singing a pro-IRA song! And I am the only person joining in.

It was time to get the hell out of there and only in the memory is it funny. At the time, it was knife edge stuff. But everywhere I went in Ireland there was similar craziness. You can call it character, personality, local nuance but it was always bonkers.

Next stop Mooncoin – literally in the middle of nowhere and not an arsonist in sight to get you there. But, it was a good friendly pub, full of nice people who knew their darts.

Again, the Irish had a sense of stage and in-joke about them.

One of the locals kept saying to me the same thing over and over again:

'You keep playing Burgess, Taz will be here in a minute.'

Should it not be the other way round? Taz keep playing and the former World Number Three will be here in a minute. One thing was for sure, they rooted for their own round here until you could turn them on a comedy moment.

10 pm comes. Taz walks in. Well, I assumed it was him.

Curly hair. Odd looking. I could see he was nuts in an instant. Obviously, I was now quite experienced in identifying those slightly short of a few up top. This guy was clearly something of a legend in these parts. You just got wise to it. You knew that the whole week people were talking him up and counting down to the local showman taking on the pro with absolutely nothing to lose and everything to gain and dare I say it – a walk on that put some pros to shame!

But it was all a bit bizarre – dodgy, weird, and totally nonsense.

My – did this man know how to make an entrance. He strolls in with a huge doll – yes, a doll – of a Tasmanian Devil then places it on a chair, facing us underneath the dart board.

He was billy bonkers. This is clearly not the first time *he* has done this. I didn't dare ask if he had a history with arson, for fuck's sake. I think the locals had seen this a million times before too when there was visiting 'hospitality'. It was like being in some voodoo show in New Orleans – not that I have ever been to New Orleans obviously but I have seen the James Bond film set there so it must be real!

We were due to play the best of three. Of course, I didn't know at this stage if he was any good with the arrows or just completely off his head.

It was the latter. The local mad man had been entrusted with darts. You still had to have your wits about you. It was not the same in any way as Phil's driver getting me the Port and Brandy but it was clear that whatever level of darts you played, gamesmanship, showmanship and bullshitship – a word I have just made up – were totally part of the armour. If somebody got under your skin and that made its way into your mind, you could be so distracted that before you knew it, you were packing your bags and on the way home.

Unfortunately, Taz, you did your best mate but it wasn't coming anywhere near me even on a shite day!

I needed 80 to win. Double Top straight in. Now, time for some fun. I threw the next one straight into the head of the doll between the eyes. *I* didn't bat an eyelid. I was letting everyone know that I could throw a dart wherever I wanted and I was putting down that marker that you can shove your silly little gimmicks where the sun doesn't shine.

Next, of course, I threw Double Top again. You could hear a pin drop. Nobody said a word. It was all very well at exhibitions like this playing the joker and bantering with the crowds but at some point you had to show some class, and always mindful of the fact that they would remember one great dart, I gave them their moment on a plate.

I walked towards the doll, pulled the darts from its head and turned to Taz.

'Don't worry mate,' I told him. 'It's only a joke, it's just an exhibition.'

But it wasn't. Little did I realise that I had taken a red rag to a bull...or indeed a doll.

The next thing I know Taz is walking up to the doll. He sticks his hand up its backside. Then, something I have never seen before... I guess the locals knew what was coming. He pulls out a gun from inside the bloody doll.

Now, he's coming my way and holds the gun to my head. I can feel the cold steel of it against my skin.

'You're not fucking laughing now are you?'

Geez – all the blood drained from my body and I am thinking 'this is it, this nutter is going to fucking shoot me.'

He stands there for what must have just been a few seconds but of course felt like a lifetime with everybody staring to see what happens next. He pulls the gun away, shoves it up back up the doll's arse and marches to the bar. The Irish music booms out again and the room collapses into laughter.

Choreographed. Everyone in on it.

I reach for a chair and need at least a quarter of an hour sitting down to take it in properly. To this day I still don't know if the gun was real or not.

He was always going to do that. He wasn't even there for the darts because he was pretty rubbish. But this was his party piece and the crowd knew it too. It was all about the reaction and I took the bait. God only knows what they said about me after I had left. And I am sure his next victim came along the week after. I never saw him again thankfully.

Once I recovered from my near-death experience, I looked up and couldn't spot him anywhere. All part of his act, I'm sure, but he had vanished into thin air. Let's hope an arsonist gave him a lift home!

Once my veins stopped throbbing, I actually felt regenerated – almost super human. When you are literally staring down the barrel and come back from the dead, you will have to trust me on this one...you do feel a million dollars.

And I had to go again. The music was pumping. But I found a second wind – or I needed to just show them that I wasn't some rollover and die character. I don't know what kicked in but I was instantly taking the darts a lot more seriously. I was in the zone. Suddenly, I was hitting everything in sight, playing out of my skin.

As was tradition, I was due to play the landlord last. It was as though as they had done their homework on me. Out came the dry ice and through it he emerged dressed as Phil Taylor, wearing a cape and walking on with Phil's music. Only the bloody Port and Brandy were missing.

We were playing best of three. The first leg, the landlord needed 153 and I just wanted Double Top. I was cruising. Then, as if I hadn't seen enough tricks, the chalker who was keeping scores, pipes up and tells us to swap darts.

'You're not throwing your darts anymore,' he ordered.

I was throwing standard flights and my opponent was chucking these long missiles that weighed a ton. Destination unknown.

'Swap darts and swap score,' he added.

The landlord misses Double Top with my darts.

No problem. Treble 20, Treble 19, Double 18. Boom.

The landlord gives me my darts back.

Second leg.

Next, he needs 161 and I just require Double Top once more.

Same again.

'Swap darts. Swap scores.'

This time I am to exchange with the chalker.

He tells me mine are too easy to throw. His are like chucking scuds.

The landlord misses again.

Bang. Treble Top. Treble 17. Bullseye.

On. Fucking. Fire.

I had never thrown anything like that in my life. I had made similar finishes but arrows that weighed a ton were new on me. I might have looked a mug earlier with the bloody Tasmanian Devil but now I was giving them what they really came to see. I left them spellbound. It was really important to be able to take a joke on a night like this but also embed in them that you were some sort of darts god even if you weren't! Whatever they chucked at me, I just lobbed it back.

A terrible night turned out to be brilliant. You were supposed to play no more than sixteen people. I would play everyone in the pub! Sometimes, I would have 30 matches. I didn't care. £300 a night was enough to stick the fuel in the car and plus – double bonus – I got out of there alive.

Ireland constantly produced the best memories, greatest jokers and the best stories. Sometimes the joke was on them though.

I had been given this really expensive bottle of brandy in a box. It must have been worth £100 or so. I had long since drunk the brandy but was still carrying around the box. I had been packing up the campervan when I thought for a laugh I could use it as a gimmick and offer it as a prize to anyone who could beat me on the bullseye in an exhibition.

So, I inserted a brick in the box and sealed it up. Pick it up and it felt like a bottle of brandy! I hadn't thought it through.

This lasted for a few nights.

I pull a name out of the hat and this old boy comes up to the board. He nails the bullseye first time. It has never happened to me before. Gimmick over in an arrow. I am stunned. Everyone is cheering and applauding. I have no choice but to present it to him.

Obviously, I am literally bricking it!

I allow a few moments to pass and then wander over to the table to have a few friendly words. I tell him it is a very expensive bottle and to not start opening it up in here of all places – save it for Christmas.

Then I think a little later that I really need to go and have another word. I will play a couple of people and then pop over when it is quiet.

I turn round and there is nobody there. The table has gone. I am asking everyone where the old guy is but he is nowhere to be seen. I am guessing he is thinking his night does not get much better than this. Until he gets home. If it had been some cocksure pissed up young'un who had been heckling me all night, I probably would not have thought much of it but I did feel really bad and I know now that this is one book that particular gent won't be queuing up to buy. Unless he is still saving it for another Christmas and still hasn't opened it. People do *do* that.

Every town left a story.

I was due at an exhibition in the North. So many miles and so many towns…so many beers and so many nutjobs…I can't even remember its name. It was a pretty normal night following the usual sequence of events for a gig. But I was starving and had barely eaten all day.

We were also in a rough part of the country. There had been so much fighting in the pub's toilets that the wall had been knocked through and replaced with a massive Perspex sheet. That meant only one thing. When you were having a piss, everyone at the bar was watching. Classy joint.

I asked the landlord if I could find something to eat nearby.

'Nothing round here,' he brushed me off dismissively. 'Can I do you something? I can do you a steak and some onions, if you like.'

So I accepted but he told me he couldn't do fries! He wasn't firing up the kitchens just for me. It was like nobody had ever eaten here before. Ever. In the history of time. Not once. Not ever.

So, I leave him with my order and play another couple of punters. I go to the bog and then what do I see? My tea is being cooked on a barbecue next to the urinals. Piss is flashing everywhere. But I literally am so hungry that I could eat anything – and I mean that. He had gone to the garden to dig an onion up and was serving it up complete with its coating of dirt – which I then had to peel. Well, I can honestly say it was the best pissed-stained steak and dirt-covered onion I have ever had.

I had my best darts form in the North, winning the Irish Classic twice against quality opposition including Jamie

'Bravedart' Harvey and Alan 'The Iceman' Warriner. The Split, of course, made you question the value of a title even more.

Not only were the governing bodies at war and you weren't sure what was being wiped from the records but there was now possibly double the number of tournaments and you could collect tin pot trophies for fun if you manipulated your tour and your exhibitions.

But a title is a title and the Irish Classic *was* worth winning and you can only play who you are drawn against. There is all the space in the world on Wikipedia but if says you won the Irish Classic twice, who gives a sod about the background?

I have just fucking checked. It doesn't say I won it at all!

At the end of the day, career stats are for looking back on. In the moment that you produce them, you just wanted to be in form, get pissed and walk away with more cash than you were getting before. You are on a treadmill.

You can probably see then that Ireland was good to me though in so many ways. Not only did I pick up a few worthless pieces of tin that would get less than a whoopy cushion on the *Antiques Roadshow* but it was always a carnival that sharpened your wit, banter and sense of performance and provided lifelong memories of being 'on tour'.

And as we all know, what goes on tour stays on tour…until you are broke and need a book out!

My six week jaunt concluded with the Second World Grand

Prix in Rosselare. Another world tournament! Location: a marquee on a hotel car park. I turn up in the worst possible conditions. These were the strongest winds Ireland had ever known in 25 years.

This is where Mick showed his genius.

So, he came to me about the walk on music – which of course is now an integral part of darts.

'Purple and Gold,' he told me. 'You walk on to Purple and Gold.'

'What the fuck is Purple and Gold?' I asked.

'You walk on in Ireland to Purple and Gold.'

Non-plussed, I just agreed.

'Every county in Ireland has its own anthem. We are in Wexford and here it is Purple and Gold.'

I didn't have an alternative and I didn't know better.

'Trust me,' he assured. 'Everybody in this tent will be on your side.'

I think it is the local curling song.

Mick was conjuring up a real sense of drama. I march on in front of 4500 people in the tent and people are crying. You could feel the emotion. The whole place is in tears and I didn't even know what they were fucking crying about. This was a genius move from him.

It fired me up too. In impossible conditions with the marquee just about hanging on in the gales, I whipped Alan Warriner in a rip-roaring Quarter Final, never threw a bad dart against Peter Manley, destroying him 6-0 in the semi and then was facing guess who in the final.

This was great news for my good friend Billy O'Brien who had £50 at 66-1 that I would win by that score.

I chose to avoid Phil beforehand this time. When I came on to Purple and Gold, the whole room was now in overdrive. Mick *was* a genius. I thought this time would be different. The atmosphere had revved me up too. Phil was on fire though, tearing into me. He won the first set to take an early lead. At 2:1 I needed a piss and there was a three-minute loo break. The only problem was the toilets were miles away and everyone was heading there. There was no choice but to pee out the back up against the tent in full view and in full face of the roaring winds. So, I did. Out the back and up my entire fucking trouser leg. World Number One versus World Number Three and he is gonna beat me with my trousers stinking of piss.

That summed it all up. Even in my prime, I still couldn't take him. Phil was the first to take it *really* seriously. We all thought we could beat him. He showed us up for what we really were...trying to drag ourselves into the professional age but actually not really taking it seriously enough.

He had the edge on us all. In every sense. Psychologically. Preparation. Performance. The only word I could muster, beginning with P, was the one running down my leg.

<u>Chapter Seventeen</u>

Paddy and Murphy

Well, actually, as I title this chapter with a dated Irish reference, I should just point out that there is no Paddy. Just Murphy. Big Jack Murphy. Jack was still a very competent player in his 60s and I only met him through the darts. That was life on the road for you. I was staying at his. This could only lead to one outcome. Utter carnage.

You can probably write the next words yourself. Yes – obviously we had been in Billy O' Brien's pub all night! Billy and Jack had become my best friends from Rosslare.

And when I say we were staying at his...what I actually mean is that I was sleeping in the van in his back garden. This is an important detail.

Firstly, when you think of Phil rocking up and parking his campervan near the TV trucks and me finding a side lane for the night, actually pulling up in somebody's green and promised land was as close to home as you can get.

That whir of traffic was gone. You could always wander into the house for some milk or a proper shower or company. You were on holiday, working.

Plus, this was Ireland and if you are smart enough to have worked out that if I was parking in his garden, then you probably have realised that this was not a street of terraced houses.

Nothing but land all around. No neighbours therefore. Well, not quite. Is this a good time to tell you that up to now I had never eaten hare before?

It was the first thing that struck me. It was Jack, myself, and a field full of hare. There was more hare there than on his head.

'Is there any chance we can shoot a hare sometime?' I asked him, as I felt my plan forming.

It is now 2 a.m. The booze was talking. So was the belly.

Jack was thinking slightly differently:

'We'll go and get one now if you like. I'll get my boy out of bed.'

The next I know, he is firing up the old Honda Accord and his lad is sat on the bonnet…in the middle of the night…with a pissed up driver. The kid is holding the shotgun. I am speechless.

But highly entertained.

They make it about a quarter of a mile up the road. Let's be honest, what the fuck did I know – two things go immediately with booze – no sense of time and no sense of distance!

I am staring at the boy through the windscreen. It is wet as usual in Ireland. The fields are sogged right through. Suddenly, the boy throws his hands on the glass. This is a signal to stop the car. Hares hunched down in face of the headlights of the car remain motionless.

Boom. A shotgun resonates all around the hills. It was the kind of place where you could hear a pin drop at night so you can only imagine what the sound of the cavalry was like. I couldn't believe it was actually happening. But then again, of course I could. Jack was as mad as a hatter and this was the hatter's tea party. We all were bonkers. I didn't expect him to be out at two in the morning shooting his neighbours' hares.

Boom. The shotgun was still echoing. Then I saw what we had plundered. It was enormous – the size of a Jack Russell. And the lad flung it straight into the back seat of the car.

It was so natural. It looked like they had done this a thousand times before – as though my jokey request was not unusual. Then they set off again. Hey, why stop at one? Second one. Boom. Straight in the back. Fuck it. Why stop at two?

Problem. The car is stuck. The wheels are spinning. The shoot is over before it begun. We are now going nowhere fast. Two down, plenty to go but the remake of *Watership Down* was now becoming *The Tortoise and the Hare*.

This is all we need. I know the firing of a shotgun in the middle of the night is enough to set alarm bells ringing but a breakdown in a field will wake up the entire neighbourhood. Especially, if you are pissed.

'Don't worry, I'll get my tractor and pull it out,' said Jack calmly.

It must have been nearly 3 a.m. I could tell this was not as unusual to him as it was to me.

'I can't leave my car here,' he stated, about to deliver another curveball. 'It's not my field.'

Oh fuck. Pissed. Firing into the night sky. Kid on bonnet. Dead hares in the back. *Hairs* standing on neck. And now someone else's land. Presumably too, someone else's hares not that hares are family pets. We have a mile or so walk back to Jack's house.

His lad runs off ahead of us down the road.

'Where's he going?' I ask.

'My starter motor doesn't work in my tractor,' Jack attempted to improve the night! 'My boy has gone to borrow the neighbour's tractor.'

Oh fuck. Borrow meant steal, of course.

'They normally leave the keys in it,' he attempts to re-assure me. 'It will be fine.'

I am just left to stand there. Once you have made a few pissed suggestions as to how to get this show back on the road, you don't half sober up quickly when you've dead hares in the back of a stuck car with the prospect of a stolen rescue vehicle on the way whilst your shotgun cartridges resonate into the night sky.

We could be here all night.

Tractor one comes round the corner!

Jack starts linking up the chains from the tractor one to tractor two. In the middle of the night. Pissed. He gives us the sign that we are ready to go. Thank the Lord.

We set off down to find the car.

In the field, we hook the chains up from tractor two to pull the car out of the mud. Jack's lad has set off to return tractor one.

But no, could anything else go wrong? Yes – we are just about to pull away. Shit – we are out of diesel. This can't get any worse. The car, the tractor and the lot of us would be heading to prison if we did not sort this mess out by first light, or if we just got really unlucky and – albeit in the land of the lock-in – those friendly cops who wander into the pubs after dark and leave pretending that there is nothing going on might not turn a blind eye now.

Car and tractor are now stuck in the field!

You know it is a race against time but you simply don't know how much time you have, or indeed what the fucking time is. By 5 a.m, we just give up. Sod it, we'll go to bed. It is too late now when in reality it is too early.

I grabbed the hares from the back seat and we trudged back to Jack's. We'll sort it tomorrow but again, actually today. While we were sleeping, everyone else would discover the destruction we had abandoned.

I still had time to skin the hare in the garden of course before

117

hitting the sack. I left the next morning like a coward fleeing the scene of the crime. I won't be back here anytime soon – I reasoned – Jack knows these people round here and what goes on. He can sort it. Local rules apply.

Another day, another town and after spending the next 24 hours shaking my head first piecing it all together then wondering how we got into such a mess, I soon forgot about it. If you don't hear of any drama in the following couple of days, you tend to think it has got sorted. Anyway, as I said, I wouldn't be back *hare* anytime soon.

Soon turned out to be four months later!

'I only got my car back last week,' Jack told me.

Chapter Eighteen

All At Sea

As hare-raising as it had been, staying at Jack's had inspired me. I was now looking at tournaments and exhibitions and packing everything I could to make a week of it. So on that trip back to Ireland the next time, I prepared like a pro.

That's right, I took an air rifle and my fishing stuff! A couple of days to kill in Ireland now had a new meaning. A couple of days to kill. If I could park up somewhere and shoot my dinner then we were quids in.

I parked up near Castlebar, in County Mayo.

I didn't have a clue where to go.

'Is there a beach near here I can fish from?' I asked a local.

They all seemed friendly enough.

'Yeah, follow the yellow signs…it won't look like you are going anywhere…when there are no signs come back to the clearing and there is a ditch. Drive across the ditch out on to the sands. Don't worry, the sands will be hard enough to drive on.'

Local rules may apply but knowledge was always king. Never mind what a map said.

'The tide goes out a mile and a half,' he added.

Well the beach seemed solid so, a touch apprehensive, I weighed it up and thought that the locals see this day in day out, twice a day so there was no point asking if you weren't going to take the advice.

So far so good. The guy was right. The sand was 'rock hard, rock solid' as he had told me, and advised to pull up 150 yards from the low tide and then if it starts coming in just to move the van back a couple of times. He clearly knew what he was on about.

I began to relax and take in the scenery and the calmness of the water thinking it really does not get much better than this.

Sometime later an English dog walker passed me.

'Caught anything yet?' he asked politely.

'Fuck all,' I responded and let out a booming laugh.

'Nice day for it, though.' He piled on the passer-by small talk!

'You never been here before?' he added.

Clearly, I hadn't, as I suspect he well knew.

I shook my head then he delivered the crushing blow:

'Nobody told you, then?'

I looked at him perplexed because nobody *had* told me obviously.

'The tide comes round behind you here and fills up that ditch.'

120

'You've got about ten minutes or so, or your campervan will only be heading one way – all the way over the sea to the USA.'

What the fuck? If I only had ten minutes then I didn't even have ten seconds to question him. I suspect he had seen it all a thousand times before too.

My God he was right. That mythical ditch was already full by the time I got there. I would guess more than full – with about 8 feet of water. I barely had time to pack up, just hurling everything in to the back of the van before speeding off back up the ramp at a million miles an hour and with no choice but to run at the ditch *Dukes of Hazard* style. I just cleared the gaping hole... but had to say goodbye to the crockery!

All the tat I had bought to eat my proposed legendary haul of hare in, went flying. Campervans are not the best full stop when it comes to speed bumps or bridges or anything on pothole road Britain. They always sound like a bit is about to fall off and even though all those cupboards are bolted down, everything rattles its arse off inside and you wonder at the best of times how stuff remains unbroken. Now, I was tearing off a beach at speed and hadn't had time to secure the contents of the van and that process included taking a running jump across the ditch. No wonder that was the end of that.

If you think of what you have to go through to pass a driving test, no part of it ever indicates that you will be in charge of a van with glass and china inside it and you will literally close your eyes, rev up speed and shout to yourself 'well here goes, wish me luck' but that is exactly what happened.

I won't draw out the suspense because I am not stupid. You are reading this book so I obviously just about cleared it, with probably a minute to spare. The end process of that close your eyes wish me luck syndrome is to then pull over, head leaning into the steering wheel and almost fake pant to yourself before uttering 'that was fucking close'...to nobody listening. Ireland had driven me potty. I now talking to myself and acting like a cliché.

I start to replay the conversation with the first guy I met. I can see him pottering off probably muttering to himself that 'the mad Englishman won't take a blind bit of notice and will probably be washed away to sea' but the truth is that he only told me half the story. All he said was to wait on the tide. He did not tell me that it comes right behind you up your arse! If it hadn't been for that chance passing of the dog walker, I would have holed up somewhere in the ocean half way to the States.

What do you do after that, then? That's your day ruined for sure. In the middle of nowhere and now distrusting of everything anyone tells you, you really did have two days to kill before time killed you.

Chapter Nineteen

MC Stands For My Cock

Even though that particular Ireland extravaganza turned out to be a fucking nightmare, I was now living the dream. You will notice that apart from the odd Tasmanian Devil here and there, I hardly mention any of the matches I play.

I will fall short of saying they were now a means to an end but if all we ever wanted was a good life and the darts to pay for it, then a good life I was now having. Obviously, if I am not recounting every bloody tournament then I am probably not quite at the top of my game but equally, you would have stopped reading by now if all I had to tell you was that I needed bullseye and Double Top but Phil still kept beating me in the final.

You probably would be right to conclude that if I am spending this much time in the late 1990s thinking of my next adventure then I was never going to be anywhere near the zone to be a force of power over The Power.

Phil was a relentless machine, practising all the time and scooping trophies and the cash for fun. Except, it was me that was having the fun and probably a bit too much. He leaves his mark as having been a great in the game. I leave my mark as having had a great time hunting game.

It wasn't just Ireland that distracted me. I used to get a lot of banter from a classic stereotypical northern audience. They gave as good as they get.

I had learnt to work closely with the MC at exhibitions – if you didn't, you were basically on your own if it went wrong, you weren't funny or started a riot. It was not just Phil Taylor who had the power. So did the man with the microphone. I became good pals with the late Freddie Cooper who had made a name for himself announcing in the Yorkshire area and was to be my MC for one night in Armthorpe just outside of Doncaster. I had not warned him that I had some plastic chickens rolled up tight in my pocket.

They were not left over from an England international match fee by the way.

Before the night got going, I told Freddie my plan

'When a fruity looking bird comes up, when I give you the wink, do something different,' I whispered to him. 'Announce that if she gets a ton or more, Shayne will get his cock out.'

He looked at me aghast.

'We don't do that sort of thing around her,' he cautioned.

'Trust me Fred,' I replied. 'It will all be fine. It is not what you think.'

After about four or five games, this young lady comes up and

I give Fred the wink to say 'let's do it now'. Fred is mouthing to me nervously to check I am sure.

'If this young lady scores a ton, Shayne will get his dick out,' Freddie announces apprehensively.

'No,' I mouth to him under my breath. 'I will get my cock out.'

He tried again:

'Right ladies and gentlemen if this lady scores a ton or more, Shayne will get his dick out.'

'No Fred, my cock,' I insist.

'Thee calls it a dick round here, son.'

The carefully-crafted subtle linguistic nuance was lost on him.

Fortunately, her biggest score was 85, sparing me the embarrassment but undoubtedly leaving everyone in Yorkshire thinking I was some kind of dirty freak show.

My plastic chickens and theatrically designed humour remained hidden. As did my dick.

Often it was the case that when you rocked up at these places, you were the only show in town – for months.

Of course, Friday night piss ups did have riot written all over them. The booze, the nature of the game, the ability to topple a champ and the fact that there was almost no other sport where you could get this close to a player and breathe shit in his ear...it had it all.

You always knew when it would kick off too.

I am playing an exhibition with the world-famous MC Russ Bray on the mic at the White Lion Pub in Waltham Abbey organised by Steve West. Steve is now one of *the* top players inside the Top 32 of the PDC. His brother Tony, a former World Master, was also playing. This was going to be a good night.

It was rare that *we* caused these riots, however. We were just the magnet.

Russ and I arrive at the pub and there is no sign of Tony. Steve is practising away. I ask Steve where Tony is and he assures me he is warming up down the road and would be here in a minute.

'Why isn't he here now?' I ask.

'He is actually barred from the pub. He is going to sneak in, beat you, then go.'

That's exactly what happened – except for the leaving bit. Once Tony had destroyed me as Steve predicted, he stayed for a pint.

The landlord's son, a pretty big guy, spots him and it all starts.

They throw him and his girlfriend out.

I carry on playing for a short while before the door bursts open and Tony re-enters, all fists flying, hitting everyone and everything with his girlfriend not far behind smashing up all the tables before order is temporarily re-installed, resulting in the door being bolted with myself and Steve on the inside of it. Women are screaming; men are on the floor. Tony is thrown out again.

'I can't have this,' I said to the landlord and Russ. 'Can Russ and I just have our fucking money now and you show us the back door?'

It was bedlam. And I scarpered. I have never fled a gig before or since halfway through. The Wild West came to Essex.

I still do not know why he had been barred in the first place but I guess the evidence was right before my eyes. Tony was known as The Tornado. That night he more than blew the house down.

This was of course locals' territory. You were turning up where they drunk night after night and the local rules applied. This was, without question, *the one* rule whether I was in the States or Sussex.

There was no greater example than that than at the Eastbourne Open – that world beater of tournaments.

I am with the late John Raby, the head of JR Darts. As you will soon realise, I am virtually the only person left in this book who is still alive.

In the field is a chap in a wheelchair by the name of Barry who is paralysed from the neck downwards. He has a blowpipe permanently attached to his wheelchair. With incredible skill, his girlfriend would load the darts into the blowpipe and off we go.

Puff. Treble 20. Puff. Treble 20. Puff. Treble 20.

Obviously, I had never seen anything like it. Locals had witnessed it countless times before.

He seemed to be beating everyone but had yet to play me.

Unfortunately, there was a spanner in the works. The rules of darts clearly stated that:

(darts) 'must be thrown by the player and retrieved by the player'.

By the Saturday, he got to the final of the Singles and lost but was then told he couldn't play the Sunday as he had an unfair advantage and was not adhering to the rules. I was trying to make a living so I am afraid the rules *were* the rules. So, that meant Barry had to go. He was out. They didn't let him participate any further.

I didn't see him again for about another six or seven years when I ran into him at another tournament in the village of Wadhurst, a little market town in Sussex.

He was still plying his 'trade' so to speak, though this, of course, was *my* trade. I am not controversial. It was my living.

The prize is £300. They call Shayne Burgess versus Barry.

'I am afraid I am not going to play him,' I tell the organisers. 'I admire what he is doing but he shouldn't be playing in tournaments where there is prize money.'

'I'm not chucking my mate out,' replies the man with the clipboard! 'I decide who plays and who doesn't and my decision is he is playing.

You see – local rules apply.

Everyone else had played him. I don't think *they* knew the rules. Or were turning blind eyes.

I gave them an ultimatum – either he goes or I do.

Ironically my words fell on a deaf ear:

'I am sorry, Shayne,' came the reply. 'Then Barry stays and you have got to go.'

Not for the first time, I would leave a venue only to be shafted afterwards.

Some weeks later I found out that they had written to the place where it all started for me – *Darts World* magazine, slagging me off, calling me unprofessional and saying that I had refused to play a disabled person.

Not one person ever slated me to my face about it. The truth is that I was *more* than professional because I *had* applied the rules. It actually exposed that greater inconsistency that up and down the country and all around the world there was this small undercurrent of those who didn't want their little bit of territory upset by somebody who had just happened to have a small amount of success at the sport.

I didn't behave out of malice. £300 paid my mortgage that month. That was the reality of the scenario. Of course, there is a massive gulf between somebody bitching to a magazine and trying to turn you over to the governing body. These guys just wanted to damage me and have the last word. Nobody even remembers it now…although, having just read the last paragraph, you will!

We were always playing for such fine margins that these arguments seem blatantly ridiculous but when the prizes are small but significant enough to get you by they can cause massive arguments.

One year I got the hump with Bob Bartholomew who runs a tournament at Sidley on the last Saturday every month. Bob's rules were Bob's rules and that meant that if he got sixteen entries, he would always pay out the £100 prize money.

One Saturday there were close on 20 players and as ever we are waiting for all the cheese rolls to come out afterwards when Bob hands me my £60 for winning.

Out come pizzas. Not a cheese roll in sight.

'What's this?' I ask him.

'Jackie who usually does the sandwiches is on holiday this week so we had to order in pizzas this week,' he responds sheepishly.

'You mean I bought the fucking pizzas,' I yell at him being down on my winnings.

'Well, no…' he begins to retreat.

I stormed out and never returned for another year until one Saturday I sheepishly returned to make peace with Bob. The story had become a running joke in my absence and remains so still!

130

Bob and I are good friends now.

I can confirm that pizzas have re-appeared since but not at the winner's expense!

I know it seems petty and stupid now but I guess that is what happens when the intensity of professional sport takes over.

These things were important to us, though. We were always on the make and always doing things on the cheap.

Without question, the Jersey Open in the late 90s was the best example of this. It was also one of the biggest tournaments in England. Jersey is not even in England!

Big tournaments attracted big sponsors and at that stage Embassy (fags) were everywhere. You will have seen them at the snooker too. In the entrance hall, they had some sort of promotion going on where you paid 20p and if you could score over 100 with three darts, you got a packet of 20 cigs.

Somebody gave me the tip off that these girls manning the stalls were just dolly birds (dated, sexist reference I know still with contemporary usage in the darts world!) They couldn't add up for shit nor did they understand darts.

'Just go and throw the odd treble here and there,' my mate encouraged. 'They won't be able to add it up and they will ask you what you've scored. Even though you might have scored 80 or 90, tell them it is over a ton and they will give you a packet of fags.'

So, I ended up with more cigarettes than a dodgy

supermarket run to Calais. There was only one thing to do – give them to my Pairs partner Les Baylis who proceeded to chain-smoke his way through the weekend, and of course with every fag came a pint. I was playing with the equivalent of the Canadian snooker legend Bill Werbeniuk!

Les was a good county B player but somehow found an extra gear and played out of his skin in Jersey meaning that by the close of play on Saturday at some stupid hour in the morning we had reached the Semi Finals. The longer we stayed in, the more free fags he smoked.

We were just about to leave the venue.

However, the wrong person informed us and in fact we had to go back on to play the Semi against two of the best Pairs players in the world in Ronnie Baxter and Alan Warriner.

Les can barely walk by this point but somehow we destroyed them. I think they were looking at us thinking a couple of hillbillies had just robbed them of what was rightfully theirs.

I shook their hands and got chatting but Les is nowhere to be seen. I turn round and he has literally slid down the wall and his eyeballs are round the back of his head. Only adrenaline kept him upright. It was probably the worst I have seen in a darts player and the best performance from someone in the worst condition I had seen!

He had clearly peaked though – we got battered in the final the following day.

Over the years, I lost a lot of friends from the darts world. That unhealthy lifestyle took its toll. Occasionally there was awful tragedy too. Jason Woody Wood – another bloody inspirational nickname – had become a really good friend of mine despite our fifteen-year age gap. We had met working together for Kennedy Construction digging and laying water pipes around the time I turned pro.

Woody was quite an accomplished player and an MC. He would often ring me to tell me there was an easy £100 down the road at an exhibition. It was always the same scenario. I would drive there and he would drive back. Despite being the MC, he would down more ale than me!

He might really have gone on to much better things had it not been for New Year's Eve 1999. The birth of the millennium, the death of Woody.

That night Woody had been drinking in The Wheatsheaf – my mate Cardy and *I* had pre-paid a fiver to get in The Tivoli to see in the New Year. Around 1130, Woody was trying to get in our pub but couldn't get in as it was ticket only so decided to make his way home.

At around half one in the morning, his neighbour called. She had been to Trafalgar Square but the train terminated at Sevenoaks with no sign of any cab for miles. Would he – Woody – pick her up?

So, Woody, probably a bit worse for wear, says he will drive to the station to fetch her. He had a heart of gold and would do anything for anyone. He never made it. By six this morning, people are knocking on his door. The neighbour had Finally found a taxi and blew £100 getting home.

Woody had a hit a telegraph pole in a little village called John's Cross. The car was overturned in a field and he was dead at the scene. Nobody knew anything until the next day.

To this day, over two decades on, he is still missed. It was the worst possible start to the millennium. Life is never smooth.

Chapter Twenty

Super King of Darts

The darts map was never straightforward either. A handle of counties at home embraced the sport and abroad outside of America, Canada and Oz you could never really be sure but once place that really took my interest was Belgium. Nowadays Brussels is in the news every bloody day but realistically if it weren't for Europe basing itself there politically, you would never hear of the place again.

But – it was well on my radar. There were some pretty decent tournaments out there and in the new spirit of 'have van will travel', Burgess Adventures started exploring the possibilities of the cross-channel ferries! The big gig was at a place not dissimilar to Center Parcs in the UK. Everybody wanted to play Molenheide.

You make a couple of trips. You watch the lorry drivers. You observe all these families with their cars packed to the rafters with sleeping bags and whinging kids doing word searches in the back just wanting to get on and off and to their destination at the other end. You start to come through channel ports and customs with some regularity. You realise that they barely stop you, mostly wave you on and don't give a toss about your passport.

Things are slightly different these days of course when you could get a couple of miles down the road from Dover and get a tap on the glass to find some poor displaced individuals with no grasp of English who have given away their life savings to try to make a passage to the apparently soft target of the United Kingdom. Doubtless, things will change ahead when Britain has said Adieu to the EU. Look at that, Burgess does Brexit!

But then, if I wanted to rip the floor up in the van and make use of the cupboards and panels in the toilets because frankly, officer, what else is a man supposed to do with 5000 cigarettes, then that is what I would do! You would be amazed at the amount of cubbyholes there are in a campervan. And come on, I wasn't the only one.

The whole notion of contraband has changed so much from when you would walk through Nothing To Declare knowing full well that you had bought an extra bottle of wine in from France to take you to the daredevil sum of ...something like two! The rules were flimsy then, the allowances were a joke, exploiting was a piece of piss without ever taking an amount that made you look like an alcoholic, a chain smoker or a tart that wore too much perfume and then the punishment was fuck all.

If you were going to get caught, you were going to get caught.

Nobody ever stopped me.

It had been an open secret for some time that many of the players were into a bit of smuggling and making some cash out of it. The plan was always to win Molenheide then stop on the French Belgium border at a place called Adinkerke and stock up with fags, drive to the port and flog the lot when you got home.

Of course, all the plans were now linking up. I worked in an industry – like it's a fucking industry – where old school still prevailed a little. That meant our playing field was your pub and even though I began my so-called career before the smoking ban, a lot of that club mentality still existed. But, more to the point, I had seen the way the culture around the darts evolved in Ireland.

So, get through British customs and get ready for Ireland where I knew they wouldn't search you when you drove on the ferry. The idea was hatched. My smuggling career was underway.

Now, it probably wouldn't look great to be the star turn selling fags out the back of my campervan but equally this was a place where the cops didn't seem to notice a full-on lock in and you could steal a neighbour's tractor at 3 a.m having shot the local hares and you could probably get away with it. But that was the plan. Play the darts. Open up the van!

So, as attracted as I was to Belgium for the darts, I now was thinking of a bigger picture and a triangular route involving these two countries and home. I knew everyone in Tramore smoked!

I learned my lesson early though. I hadn't done my research.

137

I would get to a tournament in Southern Ireland and half my mind would be on the darts, the other would be in setting up my little nicotine stand!

Unsurprisingly, there was huge uptake. No, that is not accurate. There was enormous *interest* but I got the wrong brand.

'You want some cheap ciggies?'

That is how the conversation would start.

'Why not, have you got Lambert and Butler?'

This was where the business plan fell apart.

'I've only got Super Kings,' I would reply.

Then it dawned on me. Nobody was smoking Super Kings. I couldn't get rid of them. I could not even give them away. I gave up trying and asking. I am left with 5000 fags in the back of my van. I was the world's most useless import and export agent. Nothing underlined this more than the fact that a couple of weeks later I was back home then back out towards Belgium and Holland again for the Antwerp Open. I booked the trip without even thinking. What the hell *was* I thinking? Not much. I boarded the ship totally forgetting that I still 5000 fags on me.

It was only when I got to Antwerp that I realised I had been that fucking stupid that I had re-smuggled back into mainland Belgium the entire stash that my lack of business nous had already entered the UK and Ireland with and with which I had been unable to part company! All the other guys are asking me if I am getting some fags on the way back. I couldn't shift the last lot.

You can guess the rest, I assume? After the tournament, I have to head back to the UK...Might as well re-smuggle them back in once more. What on earth would I have said if they had asked me about the fags? That I bought them six weeks before and couldn't flog them? They would have impounded the van.

Equally it would it have looked too dodgy to have chucked them in the channel? I probably should have.

Nobody wanted them. I didn't even smoke. I could only get rid of them by flogging them on the cheap in pubs in Hastings.

The title of this chapter defies the truth.

I was a shit smuggler and I wasn't even anywhere near the Super Kings of the darts world.

Chapter Twenty-One

In A State, In Plenty of States

It is now 2001. I am beginning to fall out of love with the game. You might well turn around and say that you are not surprised and that I have spent too long not really wearing the look of a professional sportsman – he lives in a van and smuggles fags, he gets pissed with his audience and shoots hares...Phil Taylor was not preparing like this.

Now, the problem comes of course when your form takes a dip. It is all very well when you are riding the crest of a wave, almost gliding in and out and through tournaments. You can live like a small-time, big-time Charlie, laughing at all the scrapes and old-school amateurism that I displayed in a now professional era.

I didn't really know much different. I had always been like this. The two things that I really gleaned from the era after The Split were that this was now big business with TV contracts king, and that you, as an individual, had to carve out your niche for your image. But the rest of me was preparing as though I was still going down The Nag's Head on a Friday night.

For the record, I did actually used to play for The Nag's

Head. I haven't just made that up!

The interesting point is that with the advent of satellite television, the spotlight was more constant and without being enormous, was at an all-time high. This was more important to darts than The Split itself but obviously only came about as part of the re-structuring. But of course, the first generation of players were those who straddled both eras – many of them had an upbringing similar to me. They found darts because school didn't find them. They therefore left and tried to make their way based on little life experience or education but soon did the hard yards taking any job they could and racing around the country at night to make their name.

That entire structure pre satellite TV does not leave you overnight, and the only change you would have really seen in the first crop of players was in the glee that there was Finally some financial recognition for playing the sport at that level.

It didn't mean that overnight we began to prepare differently. Phil was the game changer in that respect but as you have read, booze was still being knocked back at an alarming rate, and moral compasses were nowhere to be seen.

There are consequences for a sudden improvement in lifestyle without any significant change in culture – and one of those is what to do when it all ends.

You often used to hear of footballers who had run a pub as they had no real skills, then drunk the place dry themselves and if they 'cried' depression people would firstly have no understanding of mental health issues then and secondly could not grasp that someone who had kicked a ball around for most of their 'working' life could in any way be unhappy.

Since satellite TV came into football, ordinary players have taken a king's ransom from the game while actual superstars have rightly become so on a global level. Football does also have unions and bodies that have been addressing the social fallout from the game for some time but it is and always has been in a different league.

Darts, despite the camaraderie, is still an individual sport played largely by one person at a time against another. When it is not going so well, where does that individual retreat to? Answer: to some dark places.

So, within twelve months of the new millennium, I was having my first wobble. And of course, you only assess that decline after it has happened. You get up, you practise, you smuggle fags (!), you have a few drinks, you play a bit. You lose the odd one and you don't think much of it. That is the way it goes. The next tournament might be a couple of weeks later and the same happens. Before you know, are several months down the line and showing no sign of form and all the fun stuff you built around your game is not fun anymore.

In good times, it sits right beside the darts. I can tell you when you are flying but being heckled at 1 a.m in a dodgy Irish pub, you give it back like the best of the stand-up comedians but when suddenly, you have no idea where your next win is coming from then there is no funny banter coming out of your mouth.

And that slide is inevitable. Few, in sport go out on a high. Most decline and only then realise. I was fading and my interest in everything around the game was going too. That affects your temper, your relationships, the way you respond to everyday experiences like watching TV or eating a meal. The stuff you used to find funny now won't make you laugh in a million years.

It is exceedingly hard in real time when you are living it to say that a particular moment was *the* moment that broke you. I also believe that you quite often don't go all the way downhill in one go. You can have a false dawn of recovery.

So, by 2001, I had really stopped making any serious money out of the game. I certainly wasn't enjoying it – and the two are probably linked because if you are not making and you have been doing it that long, then you do tend to conclude there is no point. You can see in your head that you might be back where it all started. Maybe there is something in the way Dad just gave up one sport that was a little marker to me without either of us knowing so at the time.

I wasn't quite ready to quit yet but I seemed to know the good times were behind me. I think I was somewhere between *someone* who had glimpsed the achievable but was still very much wearing his Dad's genes.

I had become friendly with a fellow PDC pro called Steve Raw from Barnard Castle in County Durham. Steve was a pretty decent player. One day he called me out of the blue. In turned out that for different reasons, he was in a not so dissimilar place to me.

'Any work down your way?' he asked.

He had just split up with his girlfriend and had moved back in with his Mum.

'Not really,' I replied. 'I am doing a few tournaments and I've got some cash in hand work.'

That was enough for Steve. He really was prepared to consider anything now his life had been turned upside down. He just had about had his train fare and not much else so I said he could stay and before I knew it, we were living in each other's pockets. And Steve was playing really well at the time.

The contrast has never left me. I was checking out of darts, wondering about and wandering about life. Steve had the same emotions but he *could* tunnel them into playing. My love for the sport had turned sour. I couldn't pull myself together by getting it back and that meant I wasn't really much good in a relationship. Steve now had no partner now but somehow found comfort in finding form.

If I am looking for that turning point, it may be the World Matchplay in Blackpool – and when I say turning point I do not mean the moment I clicked *back* into form. This was the biggest

144

reality check of where my head was at. This was when I think I knew.

Steve wasn't playing but had stayed in my room with me on the sea front. I was drawn against Nigel Justice in the First Round. Nigel had been on a good run of form. But, I expected to beat him anyway. There is the first lesson – beware of complacency nipping up on the blindside when your game is about to fall apart. If I had been paired against someone I perceived to be tougher then it might not have happened.

But I was shocking and Nigel beat me in what has to be one of the worst games there had ever been in the Matchplay. It was one of the most shocking games of my life – even the fans were queuing up to get out and out was where I was...in the first round, going down 10-5.

It wasn't even close. I was distraught like I could not recall being in any other occasion. Even when Phil had set me up with the Ports and Brandy, I was just disappointed but with the knowledge that I lost to a better player and that dissatisfaction was not at my own game but at my own stupidity.

Now, I was out before anyone really noticed and had done so on a very big stage. I walked back to the hotel in a daze. I wasn't questioning whether it was all over but knew it was all wrong.

Steve could see it too and I am really glad that he was there. I am not the kind of person to ball my eyes out at losing a darts match but I was pacing up and down swearing to myself and really struggling to get my head around it and I think it is that reaction which is key. Anybody can have an off day – and I still knew that as much as the next guy. There will always be underdogs and giant-killers. The next new kid on the block would at some point make Phil look normal. Eric hadn't been great forever but, in his day, he looked like he had re-invented the sport. This all happens and each of us knew it. But I had played shit like the wiring in my head had just been re-organised and I was reacting to it inside in a way that was new territory.

Of course, I couldn't analyse it at the time but I see it clearly now. This was a gentle sign telling me that if the game weren't up yet, it soon would be.

Steve knew me just about well enough to see these were unchartered waters and from nowhere pulled a rabbit out of a hat. Rather than a field.

'I've managed to save a couple of quid…shall we fuck off to the States for a couple of months?'

The desire to flee seemed a saviour. I had had this kind of invitation once before you will recall but now, while a true pro's reaction would be to guts it out and come back, I simply said yes.

'We'll get the tickets, pick up a cheap car, go to tournaments and come home when the money runs out,' Steve finalised the details out loud.

It just goes to show that when they say that 'a week is a long time' in politics or sport or anything there is some truth in it because by the time the World Matchplay was ending, we were landing in San Antonio, Texas.

Steve had made contact with a lady called Becky Shamblen who, along with her mother Carol, kindly picked us up and showed us round. It did work a bit like that once you had been on the circuit a few years, and we were able to stay at her parents' trailer van park for a week before we decided the 'holiday' was over and that we had better hit the road and earn some money. Rock and roll!

We had hired a car for six weeks, knew we had to do this on the cheap and Becky and her Mum worked out a vague itinerary of tournaments – was there any other professional sport in the world where you could just virtually turn up and play? There are so many rules and qualification criteria in every field but in darts you could walk out of one tournament (technically I was dumped out), get on a plane and drive yourself to another whether they were expecting you or not!

That driving was down to me – Steve had no license and gone were the days when either of us didn't consider that a problem. He was also a chain-smoker which meant that I inhaling about 40 fags a day. I didn't have the heart to enquire for my own amusement if he had liked Super Kings.

America though, held tournaments almost every week of the year. Darts were slightly different in that there were steel tip and soft tip. For this trip, we were only playing steel tip. It was the place to be to earn some cash, find some form and to do it all under the radar. You could eke out a living. Most importantly, I needed a change and America was it.

Wherever we went we got that 'ringers' tag. The locals looked at us like we were stealing their money and fame. Bizarrely too – and I know it is often said Americans don't do irony – but for a country the closest to us in terms of language so much got lost in translation.

One morning, as rough as fuck in a rare McDonald's outing thinking we were about to spew green stuff everywhere, I sidle to the counter to place my order:

'Can I help you, Sir?' the spotty little teenage fucker asked.

'Just want a Coke, no ice,' I asked.

'What's ice?' he stared at me.

'Cold stuff you put in a drink,' I glared back. 'No ice.'

'What's ice?' he re-iterated.

'The square stuff in the machine over there,' I pointed. 'No ice.'

'What's ice?' he asked again.

It dawned on me we were talking a different game.

By now, a queue was forming muttering behind me at the mad Englishman.

The assistant leans over and spells it out slowly like I am a foreigner:

'What. Size?'

I *am* a foreigner, of course, but I thought we spoke the same fucking language.

'Large,' I shouted, eyeballing him up close to his face.

You can see why I don't go to McDonald's very often.

We really were doing it no thrills, checking at motels, where they were surprised we didn't want the hourly rate, often paying just $20 a night. At one seedy joint in Baton Rouge, Louisiana, we shared our first-floor apartment with a frog on our TV and crickets in the bed. Think of the worst trailer trash motel you have seen on an American TV show – normally one of those crime programmes where the local serial killers lived – double that and you have a snapshot of the kind of place we were staying – and often.

On we drove to our first tournament in Little Rock, Arkansas where nothing has ever happened except that Bill Clinton was once Governor. Well, when Steve won the Singles at our first outing, it was time to upgrade. The Best Western looked like The Ritz to us so we duly checked in.

Everything we won, we threw into the same pot and shared. I was in charge of the money.

In Lexington, Kentucky, I won the Cricket Singles and Steve won the Pro Singles. We were even beating the Yanks at their own games.

But of course, it didn't last. At one point, down to our last $100, we booked the open-ended return portion of our flight.

'Steve, we've fucked it,' I told him, counting the money.

We should have stayed in the Frog and Cricket Motel more often and let's face it, The Best Western was not the best hotel in the world. It was just a reward and an escape from the worst one.

'Unless we do something this time, we are gonna have to go home,' Burgess Travel's Treasurer announced.

We hadn't even made six weeks and the end looked in sight. Our momentary respite from our mutual doom and gloom was coming off the rails. Neither of us wanted to go back to England.

Despite what you might like to think, fairy tales do not happen in sport. The guy down to his last dollar does not win a million in the casino in Vegas.

We only went and pocketed $1000 at the next tournament! We *were* back. Stupidly giddy at returning from the dead, we bought a four-litre bottle of Jack Daniels and demolished the lot in one go. This was not good at all. A drive to Boston followed where we won fuck all, almost seeing us back to where we were financially and then we flew over to Houston for three to four days.

In an instant it became the worst possible time to be in America…

Houston, we have a problem.

Steve and I had hired a twin room and were just resting after the drive. We were due to fly on to Melbourne, Florida that morning and take our chances. Motel life was pretty grim in

150

America. They were by nature, rest points near a 'motorway', I think. I had never yet stayed in one where there was anything near you would want to visit except the fast road out of town. I am sure most people just switch the endless mindless TV on and lie on the bed before moving on again, unless you were in that weird category where you actually were – God forbid – resident! Give me my campervan back every day of the week.

I had been stirring for about an hour and Steve was still asleep. I got up to make myself a coffee then went back to bed, lying there just killing time. Then I caught the corner of the screen. I woke Steve with a kick.

'You've got to see this,' I shook him and we both started staring at each other and then back at the telly.

'Is this real?' I asked Steve.

It seemed like we were watching a film.

The first plane had just gone into the Twin Towers in New York. They were reporting live from the scene and live from the sky. Nobody seemed to know what was going on except that it looked like one of the worst accidents in aviation history. Then we saw the second plane go in.

Like many people on that day, we sat bolt upright, speechless as a fixed glaze fell over our faces. What the hell *was* going on? Certainly not an accident. Of course, the first plane attacked at just before 09H00 New York time. I don't know what hour it was by the time we decided we should get the hell out of there. We just sat there, transfixed, watching non-stop. It wasn't as though we were just watching a repeat on a news channel over and over again. New stuff was coming in all the time. Two planes. Three planes. Four. Maybe five. At one point I heard nine.

'America is under attack. Stay in your homes. Red alert.'

The TV boomed out the warning. The ticker tape bar at the bottom of the screen carrying the same line and nothing else. I had never seen anything so dramatic. Americans do tend to get more hysterical than the Brits and I know when 7/7 came similar advice was given around London but the world had seen nothing like this. We had grown up with IRA bombs in the UK, especially on my doorstep in Brighton, and witnessed the Falklands and Gulf Wars from a distance but there had never been anything like this. After the second plane, you just thought 'what else is coming?'

It was quite rare then for a first terrorist attack to be followed straight by a second one but once two planes had ripped the heart out of America you started to think the possibilities were endless.

Steve and I looked at each other and no words needed to be shared. We knew we had a plane to catch.

We packed up the little stuff we had and within minutes of deciding to head for the airport, we were on the highway. I couldn't believe what I saw next. Houston's freeway with what must have been about 12 lanes on it, was empty. We were the only car on the road. It was like one of those scenes they used to show you on the TV in 1980s of what life would be like after a nuclear attack. A ghost town. Nobody was going anywhere. In no time, America had heeded its government warnings.

We arrived at the terminal. I have never seen any airport looking so closed for business. I had flown from some pretty provincial places in my time but this was Houston. People came from miles around to make their connections here.

'Are you open?' we asked the security guard.

'Yes, flights are going, Sir,' he replied as though it was business as usual.

On the one hand America was shut. On the other, those still at their desk were booming it loud and proud that the show must go on.

There can't have been more than ten to fifteen passengers in the entire airport. We still weren't convinced that we were going anywhere. Departures were being cancelled all the time. Of course, many planes were stranded in the sky and they had to get them down so most people at the airport were still expecting arrivals.

We had no fear at this point, though many Americans were hysterical. We just knew that if we could get through the next couple of hours, board, take off and get into American airspace – wherever that was – then we would avoid being stranded here for who knows how long.

We must have been one of the last flights to take off that day.

The only people on board were Steve, myself, the pilots and a solitary stewardess. Heaven only knows what they must have been thinking.

When we landed, we discovered something approaching the full story. We had just made the cut off point before George W Bush grounded all flights across the country and into and out of the States. To have been on the ground a few hours before and then land, to play catch up with all the information that had happened while we had been in the sky was very surreal. One minute we almost seemed in the story and then were watching it unfold.

I don't know if this changed either of our outlooks on life given that neither of us was in a great place when we got to Florida. Probably like a lot of people it affected us to that degree where we vowed to ourselves that we would be better people and make each day count and then more than likely we just carried on. I know that by the time we got to Melbourne, Florida I just wanted to play good darts even though many sporting events – big and small – as well people's own individual social calendars, were being ripped up and you couldn't find much going on in life.

But life had to go on so when it was time to play, I don't know if I got lucky, was the best player that weekend *or* the most inspired to release all that tension. I went out and won the thing, beating Steve in the Quarter Final. That was odd in itself but bound to happen at some point. Darts was the only sport in the world where you would play your roommate.

When the situation calmed down a little, we actually headed back to San Antonio for a while before moving on to St. Louis in Missouri to stay with new friends John Anderson and his partner at the time Carrie Stevenson who was one of the big female stars in American darts. The country though had changed overnight. It had lost its hustle and bustle and a lot of its bullshit.

We were observers in the biggest moment in their history. In a way I think it benefited us personally. America is all noise and hard sell, particularly in the cities. That peace and tranquillity that followed whilst it put itself back together again must have rubbed off on us. It was a moment in time that is unlikely to be repeated and I not saying there will never be another terrorist attack because there have been since and there will be again but that calming unity is something that America just never offered before. Steve and I even went out night-fishing for goodness sake. He was moving on in his own life too, more than befriending a Dutch girl in her 20s.

I am sure though that whilst 9/11 changed everything around us, it also took the heart out of this American adventure. It felt like time was running out for us even though we still had around $2000 to play with. That was not a bad steal given that we were travelling huge distances, racking up bills and there were two of us.

But something kicked in. It *was* time to head back to

155

England. So, Steve and I made our way to the airport not sure when we would be back but it wasn't the first time that this kind of road trip had refuelled the mind and body. When we got to the airport, Steve dropped the bombshell that he wasn't coming.

'I don't wanna go home,' he admitted. 'There's nothing to go home for.'

This *was* a scene out of a movie. He had left it to the very last minute to tell me. I don't even think he was struggling with his decision. I am just not sure if he couldn't work out how to tell me but he decided to stay.

I gave him all the money that was left and told him he was playing really well but should have it because he might need it some day and then we said goodbye and I turned round and headed home.

I later found out he never threw another dart after I left!

I conclude that we had helped each other enormously. That trip was probably exactly what I needed at that time to stop me quitting but looking back I know now it was delaying the inevitable.

For Steve, he was right. What was there to go home for? He had met a new woman, was living in the sunshine and was making enough to survive. You get one shot at life and maybe 9/11 had told him that in a way he couldn't quite express to me. It didn't matter. In that particular moment, I understood and thought it was probably the right thing to do.

But I can tell you that there is nothing worse than coming off an American road trip turning up at places you have never heard off, beating the locals out of sight and walking into the sunset with their money than coming home to a dreary bloody Heathrow on a chilly Autumn day and wondering just where you stood in the big scheme of things.

I was soon to find out – and I was not talking about my world ranking, or any fallout from The Split, nor I had been spectacularly uninvited from tournaments that I had frequented for years.

Have you ever had that feeling of dread when you drive into your street after being away for some time and all you can think is what shit the postman has dumped on your doorstep?

Well, as I said goodbye to Steve, I could not imagine I was saying hello to the most almighty dump in history from the most enormous of heights.

I turned the key of my flat. There was a letter sleeping on the mat. It looked like it had been there for some time. The very next day, as fate would have it, I was due at a tribunal. The letter was from the PDC.

And I had to defend myself the following morning.

The accusation. I was guilty of match-fixing.

I was facing a life ban.

Chapter Twenty-Two

Cheat

Well, let me tell you there is nothing that sends you crashing back down to earth more than reaching onto the door mat to pick up an official letter telling you it is over and you are possibly a criminal when you have not even crossed the threshold of your home, having just stepped off a plane from the States.

I was stunned. I was effing and blinding round the room, slamming the letter down then picking it up and pacing up and down. I hadn't even unpacked my meagre possessions.

Then I started to wonder how long this letter had been there. There's me watching 9/11 or swigging Jack Daniels in The Cockroach Hotel and all this is being plotted behind my back. Letters like this don't just appear, they take a considerable amount of scheming and digging back in to the past, and you are the last to know.

Talk about coming crashing back down to earth with a bump.

What the fuck was I going to do? I admit I was a criminal but the letter was not coming from Customs and Excise about a shipment of fags nor was it from the National Air Rifle

Association – if such a thing exists!

I can't tell you how many times I re-read the letter. You don't take it in on the first couple of scans. It looked like it had sat there for six weeks.

I could bring a lawyer...the tribunal was tomorrow...I sharpened my senses. This was either a massive cock-up from the sport that paid you in chicken dinners or it was a witch hunt. Somebody wanted to take someone down to make a statement. The small cocks were back.

Of course, I was jetlagged too so that didn't help getting my head down in preparation for the next day. But I awoke and jumped in the car and drove myself to the venue. You can probably imagine the car journey. I am knackered, dealing with idiots on the road and the whole time having sporadic flashbacks to random points in my career where I just wonder if anyone saw anything dodgy, and then I would jerk myself back to reality by realising that my whole fucking memory was shot to pieces with all the boozing on tour.

There could well be some questions that I had a legitimate reason for not being able to answer. That might lead to suspicion. Their first offering was a gentle lob though and I made a firm statement of intent:

'Have you any representation?' Tommy Cox asked from a panel consisting of original PDC members.

'I've not had a chance,' I reminded them of something they

probably knew – that I had been away.

'I don't need any,' I confirmed. 'I've done nothing wrong.'

Of course, every player under suspicion would set their stall out like that from the off. Over the years there had been a few whispers that certain players had thrown the odd match and you are tempted to say there was no smoke without fire but remember too, that darts is a very small world once you penetrate that elite circle and there was now more TV coverage than ever (so, greater scrutiny) but the facts remain that nobody had ever been taken to court over it.

I suspect too that it is one of those things a governing body can throw at anybody at any point. The process racks up bills and time and the individual remains with a cloud over them for that entire duration and when they are (more than likely) cleared nobody hears or is interested in the milliseconds it takes to say not guilty, and in today's world Google could kill you too as the slur remains.

Just like all those press stories that splash on a front page and turn out to be bollocks only for the apology to appear on page 25 at the bottom in the corner which nobody reads, the Internet wouldn't let something like this go.

They began gesticulating like a load of old women waving bits of paper in the air.

'Do you know anything about this sum of money?' they asked.

They say you should never ask a question unless you know the answer to it, so what did they think was the likely outcome?

'What about this bet here?'

How the hell was I supposed to know what bets people were putting on in my matches?

I felt I was being carved up. Despite the huge sums of money paid to lawyers during and after The Split which tried to send out a message of some sport of spine, there were still a lot of whispers and meetings behind closed doors and you always felt that either organisation could turn you over in an our word against yours scenario.

Now it was their word against mine – or rather somebody's I had never met who had once placed a bet.

I am now pouring with sweat. As it unravels before me, I realise what I am facing. When you get that sense that this is only going one way, the voice inside your head just keeps saying 'lifetime ban'...'you're heading for a lifetime ban here'.

Then it turns out, it is multiple bets. Of course, it is. How stupid am I? No single bet would trigger suspicion but a whole load might do. Or then again, a lot of pissed people might have just fancied a certain wager that day.

Then they showed me the game in question. It was that fucking First Round exit at the World Matchplay in Blackpool. No bloody wonder. I was that shit I am not surprised that people won a load of money against me. I was odds on to win in my head at least. I didn't see it coming but maybe there is something in that that the people who run the game and those who play it have overlooked. Perhaps, the punters knew what they were doing after all!

Half of the audience turn up for a good time and drink all day and burn money at the bookies. A lot of the rest do have their favourites and their gut feelings and it is reasonable in sports like snooker, tennis and darts that a big or a biggish name falls early in the competition. That is the nature of tournament play, pressure and expectation – and probably within reason, Blackpool had my name on it. The public had proven to be wise and smarter than anybody involved in the game!

I was fucking shit and the turds that I chucked that day were the precise reason I picked Steve up on his offer and fled to the States. They can look at all the betting slips they want but they didn't see me pacing around the hotel room stressed and gutted afterwards – an exact mirror image of how I was when I returned home to get their bloody letter. They really didn't know the half of it.

In fact, as I look back on it now, most of my memories in this attempt at a book make me laugh with the sheer daftness of the situations I got into but this one makes me do so with anger. How fucking stupid was this panel? For a start, most of the bets were from people in the North East, a place I had very little association with. You couldn't get much further from Newcastle to Hastings.

Yes – Steve was from County Durham but if you have never been to Barnard Castle then maybe you won't realise that it is not part of anywhere! It is so bloody remote I am surprised it hasn't called its own referendum to leave the UK before the UK leaves the EU. If there hadn't been a castle there, there wouldn't be a town. Simple.

Ah – the parallels with Battle, just outside Hastings are greater than I thought! And I doubt for one moment that Steve told all his mates that I was firing absolute blanks and to bet against me, and even if he had then so be it.

The fact of the matter is that Geordies liked a piss up and for them Blackpool was a port of call that they had been visiting for many years. You could see the lot of them in their Newcastle United shirts on all day benders having the time of their lives. They were the epitome of the darts fan alongside all the Purfleet lot in Essex.

This bit is just for younger readers: Remember, this was the year 2001 – a few weeks before 9/11 when we were so naïve you could take a penknife on a plane! That meant amazingly, not everyone had a mobile (let alone two as they do these days), Facebook was three years away so if you wanted to know what your cat had for breakfast or see it singing Candle In The Wind you had to go and find it first rather than rely on social media, and get this, TV sport was not littered with in game betting advertisements.

I know I sound like Granddad but all the bookies handed out printed sheets to the punters. Revolutionary, I realise, but that's how it was folks. Nobody was spread betting on the phone to their broker in Mumbai. You called it as you saw it and the Geordies, through their beer goggle eyes got it spot on.

Most of their bets were in play *in* person *in print* and most of the darts I was throwing were more likely to end up in their beers than anywhere near the fucking bullseye. I was shit. They spotted it. I lost. They won. Nigel won.

That is sport.

After about 45 minutes, the panel had no option but to conclude the same. If there had been a systematic process where players were randomly called to discuss matches then I could just about accept my appearance. They *were* clearly starting to look at betting patterns but as far as I could tell I was the only person being fingered here.

If you really want to know the injustice of it all, did they call the bookies in to give evidence, was the MC or ref giving testimony, was Nigel asked to explain the game? Draw your own conclusions.

It had been a crock of shit. But let me tell you, walking away into the fresh air from the strangulation of the tribunal room and knowing that there is no case to answer is a sham – because you weren't anywhere near that status at all.

Whichever phrase you pick from 'not guilty' to 'acquitted' to

164

'let off' to 'inconclusive evidence' all come with the pre-cursor that you were 'under suspicion'. It had an effect on how people viewed you.

My fellow pros knew that I had played shit because they had all been there at some point. They also could vouch for my character – yeah, I was a bit mischievous but when you walked into the darts hall, you were a pro even when you yourself were a pissed-up pro. We all knew the line and every player creates a zone when they shoot their darts. I believed I had never met any single player who ever tried to lose and you can imagine how when you come against someone who has an edge on you or whom you just don't like, how easy it would be to start a whispering campaign that begins with the words 'I don't believe it myself but there's a rumour going round that he threw that match'.

It is simple. Anyone can light the blue touch paper and piss off into the sunset leaving the flames to douse you for any entire career. Thankfully, I received the full support from fellow players but no apology obviously from any administrator in darts.

It didn't matter. The psychological damage this had done was colossal. I couldn't shake it off and it sat on my shoulder for weeks. Experts always say that sport is played in the mind. Well, my brain was now shot to pieces.

My game went back to Square One. In effect, the American trip had been for nothing. I was at my lowest ebb. I thought

Blackpool was previously that point but the fallout from that solitary match plunged me deeper.

As time rolled on, I did begin to hear those whispers. Certain players were a bit more standoffish. It got back to me that a few thought I was a stone-cold cert to have thrown the game. Equally, I only now started to conclude that at some point most of them had a little skeleton or two in their pocket.

I also felt betrayed by the process. Unless my opponent Nigel had been called while I was in the States, I could not find any evidence that anybody else had sat before that panel. They *did* come to the correct decision. I have never thrown a match but I am sure their process was bullshit and I am convinced that they knew they had nothing when they summoned me.

If this is all part of some agenda or game, then they won. I was no longer the person nor the player I had been. All for a one-hour meeting on no basis at all. Except that I had been shit and Geordies had won money.

Nor could I see any upturn in fortunes – I started to think that the spur of the moment gesture to leave the $2000 to Steve in the States was foolish of me. It looked like I was going to need every penny I could get my hands on. Blackpool *was* a turning point but not for the panel's decision. America was a diversion that created a false comfort zone that things were actually alright. In short, it was getting to the stage where I could barely throw a dart let alone a match.

<u>Chapter Twenty-Three</u>

Do You Come From A Land Down Under?

'G'day, do you remember me…the Pacific Masters?'

We had obviously spoken then but you meet so many people at tournaments.

I had *first* met Australian Tony at the Lincolnshire Open in 2000. What a difference a year can make. I was close to the top of my game then and only lost to Mervyn King in the final.

'I was watching you but was just getting started myself. I'm the Australian rep in the BDO World Championship.' He had re-introduced himself.

I didn't really remember him at all but he seemed a nice bloke and we got talking. I don't know why he latched on to me except for the obvious reason that it must have been the darts. I would have done the same to Eric or John Lowe. The fact of the matter is that when he was just beginning, he happened to be watching me and somehow got hooked so through the quirk of life, we found each other.

'Do you fancy going for a few practices?' he asked.

'Well, I live in Hastings,' I replied, not really sure if he had heard of it or not.

He was lodging on couches in London so that was that. Nice to meet you but no can do. We did exchange numbers.

The next thing – that evening the phone rings around midnight.

It was Tony.

'Sorry to bother you, but I didn't know who else to call...' he began.

I was used to the phone going at all sorts of times of the day and night anyway with the hours that we kept but I was surprised to hear from him so soon. Nonetheless, his opening line was enough to make alarm bells ring.

'I'm a haemophiliac,' he declared.

'I have special bloods with special passes to get through customs. It has to be kept at below a certain temperature. I got home to London and the lady I am staying with has been out shopping and there was no room in the freezer for her oven chips so she has slung my meds out.'

I had never heard anything like it in all my life.

'If my bloods go over a certain temperature they are ruined and will have to be thrown away. I can't get any more in this country so then I am going to die,' he announced calmly.

Bloody hell. Cause of death: oven chips.

I really had no option but to help. Otherwise the guy was dead meat. He would be chicken fry, as opposed to chicken dinner.

I drove back to London to pick him up and brought him back to the flat I shared with my mate Neil Wallhead. We had both helped each other get on the housing ladder. Now there were three of us in this relationship!

'Neil,' I announced. 'this Aussie rang me up, His meds are in the freezer. He is gonna stay with us or he is gonna die!'

I didn't dress it up.

And that was how our friendship began, and he did become a very very good friend. He was also an exceptional player. We came to an agreement that I would do the travel and he would pay the bills and so, from the odd beginnings of him watching me in his own backyard, we became almost inseparable whilst he was in the UK.

One year he rang me up and told me he was good friends with the Australian Number One woman, Natalie Carter, a darts player from Perth. They were – like all of us – on a budget and could they *both* stay when they got back in the country. They had qualified for the World Masters and Tony stressed – separate beds. Nothing going on.

I gave them bunks and they didn't misbehave and on the day of the tournament we all drove up to Lakeside in my campervan where I was hooking up with this girl from Devon, I was sort of seeing. In fact, I hadn't seen her at all for six months! That was your darts romance for you.

That same evening Tony begins the drive home as he doesn't drink and Nat is in the passenger seat when we stop for a burger at Clacket Lane Services. Nat pulls the curtain back and I am getting down to it in the back of the van in the middle of the car park. She just stares at us.

I don't know if the brief glimpse of my Adonis figure that got her juices flowing but when we got back to mine the bunk beds became one and Natalie jumped on Tony.

Six months later, these two Aussie Number ones were married. They are now divorced. I could have told them it would never work! One and one didn't make two.

That moment aside, Tony brought a lot to my life – and much of it was very different. If you look at the mental scars that I was carrying post Blackpool, here was a guy who despite the physical tightrope he was always walking, had such inner belief that it was almost a sixth sense. In fact, it did go that far.

When you are at the top of your game whatever sport it is people will use the phrase 'eats, sleeps and drinks...' Well Australian Tony literally did sleep it and every time he would recount the dream he had.

Nor would he let it go.

'Mate, I am telling you, I have had that dream again,' he tried to convince us. 'I am going to win the World Championship.'

We would give him short change and the only reply he could realistically expect.

'Fuck off, we all dream that.'

'No,' he replied dead serious. 'All my recurring dreams come true.'

He wouldn't let it go. Of course *everybody* had that dream – hence the phrase the stuff dreams are made of. And everybody had it several times. We all did from the age of a kid to the eve of a tournament and you just kept it to yourself because it wasn't news. It happened the world over. It is happening right now. Somewhere someone is dreaming of a birdie, a Cup Final goal, the winning six.

Just, let it go.

'All my recurring dreams come true.' His recurring dream comment recurred again.

'Maybe not this year, maybe next but I am going to win it.'

I half-listened at that point because he had given himself a little reality check. He clearly understood that everyone did have dreams like that but he also knew his own mind – hence the comment that all his recurring dreams come true. He sensed he wasn't ready but it was definitely coming. To be able to put a timescale on it – as in beyond this tournament – was really quite grounded and I never forgot him saying that.

I have often wondered with people whose body does not always stand up to the rigours of life if they get something more on top. Look at the many brilliant stories of skills that autistic people have. All those billions of people on the planet and we still

171

can't crack how the brain works. All I knew was that Blackpool had wobbled me. America gave me a false high and the tribunal slashed that in half.

Here was a guy, whom I have either met by chance – or fate – who has tracked me down half way around the world, has asked me to save his life over a bag of chips who now turns out to be Mystic Meg.

We would revisit this conversation regularly but it all began to unravel in November 2002.

'Can I come straight to you?' the now familiar voice at the end of the phone began.

It was Tony. He was back in the country after a spell at home and had qualified again for the World Championships. Of course, I said yes and I could not believe the transformation in him in the previous eighteen months. He was hitting anything and everything and in my opinion was as close to Phil Taylor as you could get.

We practised together and I couldn't get near him. I don't want to even say he was on fire or playing out of his skin because that implies that he was just having a purple patch. I think now he had that focus from a long way out which I had only achieved in glimpses...or heard about in his dreams.

With my own game in decline, I think I both hid that from myself but took enormous pleasure in his rise. It is a cold hard reality check when you have somebody who has watched you and then got into the sport only to overtake you and leave you for dead in the rear-view mirror. I knew my game was slipping but for a moment when Tony was around it didn't seem so magnified.

I began driving him in my van to tournaments. He would win. I would get him home and he would give me half.

He set up a chalkboard in my lounge and one morning I asked him what it was all about. He had written 180, 160, 161, 164, 167, 170, 180.

'It's how I practise in the morning.'

He put me to shame with his work ethic.

'I have to hit all of them before I can eat,' he confirmed.

I had never thought about it any such methodical detail.

'Fucking hell,' I replied. 'I'll look like Kate Moss in two days.'

20 minutes later he had nailed the lot.

I knew he was a good player but not seeing him every week while he was away enabled me to see how far he had come so quickly. I could measure it. It was a combination of natural ability and practise. Any moment he had he would be shooting darts, joining a local league and then he was storming the Gravesend Open.

'You are Australia's best player,' a young kid approached him.

'Yeah,' he answered matter-of-factly and he knew it too.

Some people would have answered that modestly.

Australians tend to be more blunt, but he just responded almost in rhythm because his correct focus meant that he was in a zone and stopping for a tiny second to dispute that would have interrupted that.

He was so driven but not in a nasty, ruthless way. It was as though the dream was a sign from somewhere that was not necessarily spiritual but just a guide as to where he had to get to.

The kid asked him to do a 160 finish.

So, he did. 60.60. Double Top.

'Do it again,' the lad repeated.

Bullseye. Treble 20. Bullseye. No problem.

'Do it again,' the boy persisted.

'Fuck off mate.'

Which sounded worse in Australian.

Twice was playing. Three times was an intrusion. But he could deliver on cue and it left me with one thought. He is going to do this. He is going to be champion of the world.

It is the eve of the BDO World Championships 2002. Tony is listed at 100-1. This time it was me and not the Geordies with the knowledge. I was skint but could just about raise a tenner. Boom. Each way on The Deadly Boomerang.

God knows how he picked up that nickname but because of his medical condition he did have a slightly unusual action, which was partially limited as he could not bring his arm back as far as most players due to bleeding in his elbow during in his childhood causing crystallisation.

. The best monikers were admittedly all gone but the last time I looked a boomerang came back to you and that was not what you wanted with a dart.

Either way, I really was convinced. It didn't matter about the recurring dream – that was a focus for him. I could see how well he was playing and people in the local league knew too and that was an odd thing about darts. You could be on TV or in the national side but there was always a bit of local knowledge that would be unsurprised if you went from demolishing Gravesend to taking on the world in a couple of weeks.

Something had obviously happened within me too. My own decline was not on my radar. I was much more interested in Tony's game than my own and rather than taking the inspiration from it as he had with me, I stood back and admired without realising how large the gap between us had become.

Richie Davies disposed of. Marko Pusa out. Bob Taylor gone. Suddenly Tony was in the final. It was so clearly going to happen and everyone else was just late to the party, stunned how this rank outsider could just bulldoze his way through the Lakeside.

In the semi he sent home Martin Adams 5-4 and then finished off Mervyn King 6-4 to claim the title. I couldn't believe it. I *could* believe it.

I saw it at first hand from that initial meeting to the recurring dream to chalking up in the lounge. This was focus and this was star quality. The world of darts had a new kid on the block and dreams really did come true.

Such was the extraordinary character of this winner that his health did eventually fail him and after a pretty decent career, had to undergo a liver transplant in 2009. Guess what, the old bastard only went and recovered and got himself back in the Western Australian team.

I have nothing but admiration for the guy. Whether physical frailty spurred on a mental edge, or whether talent and work ethic drove him to great heights, he had something on me. But I took great pride and delight in his success.

And by the way – yes, he did walk on to Men At Work's *Down Under* and by the way his real name is Tony David.

And neither of us ate frozen chips ever again.

Chapter Twenty-Four

Share and Share Alike

This chapter comes in no particular place in my story. In fact, it comes all over the place! And that is a place I will be largely heading from now on. As the years roll by, the details loom large in my head but booze and the treadmill of tournaments mean that I can't always put stuff in the right order.

However, for the sake of these next few pages, my thought process is solely in the title and not necessarily what happened when.

I have clearly stayed in a lot of hotel rooms. For reasons of finance and to avoid the loneliness, until Phil 'moved out' to his campervan that meant we all shared rooms.

Some roommates were better than others obviously. Once in Ireland, I shared with Eric and he hardly spoke to me. Bob Anderson – The Limestone Cowboy (I know it is another cracker of a name) was always a terrific laugh.

Needless to say, whoever was companion, we all used to drink a lot. Sometimes one particular player was so pissed performing that he would unravel an entire cheap hotel toilet roll and shove it up his arse to soak up a hungover wet fart while on stage. Gross, I know, but this was televised sport and this was how professionals prepared.

Equally disgusting, a damp pump gave you some sort of comfort that it wasn't worse and in the heat of battle, you were often only thinking about how long it was until the next commercial break so you could get out to the bog. Then, it became a question of not how much toilet tissue you would need but how far down your trousers you could realistically hide it. This was not just him by the way. This was standard technique for some.

I was the floater. That meant that they would stick me in a room with anyone. Just in case you thought it referred to deposits I would leave in the bog. In time that eventually meant I shared with everyone. Generally, I would like an early night – that meant about midnight. A lot of my companions would often only function on half an hour's sleep. Darts. Booze. Kip. That was the drill. This chapter is therefore a tribute to my roommates!

Jamie Harvey, you are first! Bravedart. The nicknames show no sign of improvement.

It was the World Pairs in Bognor Regis with Reg Harding. More on Reg later…

'You're in with Jamie,' I was told.

No problem. I get to the room and he's not there.

No problem again. I will kip.

2 a.m. Problem.

Jamie rolls in steaming, chucks his bag down before he inevitably chucks everything else up. He passes out.

At 5 a.m, I wake. He is lying on the bed and hasn't moved. His $300 cowboy boots are still on. He appears dead. But is still breathing. Heavily. Like someone would who has had a few. And then a few more.

9 a.m. Sir Jamie arises. As far as the sink. At least he made it. I offer him a carton of grapefruit juice to ease the moment. He duly accepts only to pour most of it down the sink. Then tops it up with vodka. He must have lost track of time the previous evening. He is in no man's land. He stinks and he hadn't washed.

He asks me if I am coming out for breakfast. I know that I am on later that evening, and the venue Butlins piped all the games to the rooms, so I am quite happy to sit there and just watch some of the other matches.

There really was no hiding. You were in vision and you were eating in the same rooms and breathing the same air as your public. Nobody though wanted to inhale anything near Jamie that day! Jamie was sure to be no company anyway and he never returned from his breakfast.

It is now early afternoon and I awake from a little sleep and look up at the TV screen. The first Pairs game is due on. I can hear the announcer booming out.

'Please welcome on stage Keith 'Killer' Deller and Jamie

Harvey'.

This I must see. There he was – no doubt rough as a badger inside but looking with it on the screen. They must have called him, I am thinking. There is no way he got there on his own and on time. In effect he had gone straight from a night out onto the stage, with just a bit of fuel taken in, which somehow he managed to keep down after a Vodka breakfast.

Of course, they won, didn't they! And let's not forget we are talking about the 1983 World Champion in Keith. I would be lying if I said I had no idea how he did it. We had all been there. This was how it worked. At some point each of us were carrying baggage from the night before but found a way to deliver.

We roomed together again in Bognor's twin town. Alright, I lie, it was Las Vegas.

Vegas is such a timeless hot place. I don't know if things have changed but there never used to be any clocks in the casinos, and of course it comes alive at night. They create a timeless culture where you can gamble 24/7. We were always knackered after the flight and generally I would stay in the first evening. A jet-lagged body sat well in the city where time meant nothing.

I persuaded Jamie that pizza in the room was the best option but I only went an ordered an extra spicy one, covered in jalapeños. A massive sixteen-incher and the hottest kick you have ever tasted. He warned me not to eat all those green chillies, they were not good for me and that with all the dehydration after the flight and the heat of the desert I would make myself ill if I wasn't careful.

The next morning, Jamie announced that he was going for a walk down the strip for breakfast. For some stupid reason, I had picked up a face pack before the flight out. Well, the actual reason was that Boots The Chemist had a special on where if you bought nine mini travel items you got the tenth one free and I was up just short so a face pack it obviously was, just to make the numbers up. Clearly, an essential part of a darts player's kit.

I thought he would be gone for a couple of hours so – fuck it – I would give cosmetics a go. I had zero experience or knowledge of what to do. My face turned a disgusting luminous green. That alone should have been enough warning to duck out.

My skin starts to go all tight. I am stood on a chair opposite the air con trying to dry it off.

Suddenly Jamie re-enters the room. If you caught the moment on camera you would have concluded that I had secret fetishes and was not the heterosexual I claimed to be.

'I told you those fucking chillies would make you ill, didn't I?'

I could have bluffed it out but the remains of the packaging were everywhere and I knew I was done for so I confessed that I had taken to female product! That cheered the little fucker up I can tell you. I pleaded with him not to tell anyone. He assured me it was between the two of us.

He would have fallen off his chair if I hadn't been standing on it but I had given him a perfect open goal to slaughter me and by the time we turned up to play word had spread that I was not the man I claimed to be. Everyone seemed to know now that The Bulldog only got his good looks by wearing a face pack every morning!

Jamie, if you are reading – it was just the once, love and proof that if you had a story on them, they had one on you.

Everywhere I went something seemed to happen. I don't know if it was me and my personality, the nature of the people I was knocking around with or an obvious by-product of 20 or so overweight darts players who liked a drink but were bored shitless in between tournaments. Quite possibly, all of the above.

I got to room with one of my great heroes, Jocky Wilson, in Chicago. One minute you are watching them on TV, the next you are tucking them in for the night. By this point Jocky had been off the booze for three years. I couldn't imagine playing without something to drink. Jocky knew that any trip on tour was potential to lead him astray. So, we are lying there in our pants, as you would expect from two highly toned athletes such as ourselves, and I ask JW if he wants to come out for a drink.

This was a bit tight of me really knowing that he couldn't but wanted to. So, he declined and did the inevitable – lit up a fag. Picture this – two fat darts players lying in a foreign hotel room in their underpants. One lights up a fag.

Fair enough I thought, so made my way out in search of ale.

By the time I returned in a reasonable condition, Jocky was asleep. He must have gone out – dare I say it 'like a light' – moments after I left. The fag was all the way down to the butt. That is the end of the ciggie rather than Jocky's substantial arse just to be clear. He hadn't moved for hours.

God knows what floor we were on but somehow the small ash from Jocky's tobacco had narrowly failed to set his cotton sheet on fire and bring the whole house down. Different era, obviously pre-hotel smoking bans too and the automatic installation of smoke alarms!

The next day I actually draw Jocky in the first round. At the end of the game, we shake hands and he walks off.

Two Americans saunter over – big fans of Jocky but don't really know who I am.

'Hey, is that Jocky Wilson you just beat there?'

I replied that it was and – guess what – I am sharing a room with him. The next think my great hero Jocky is marching over to me and tears in to me screaming in Scottish:

'You've been fucking bad mouthing me, Burgess'

He was raging.

And I hadn't even told them he nearly set the hotel on fire!

'No-one's slagging you off,' I tried to pacify him. 'There's 800 people here to see you play.'

I would never diss one of my heroes. When he calmed down,

the non-drinking Jocky politely enquired what I was having to drink.

'A Bloody Caesar,' I confused him.

Jocky had basically been told that his liver was fucked and if he carried on drinking then that was that. Of course, he had never heard of a Bloody Caesar. Let's be honest, it didn't sound like a Jocky Wilson drink, did it?

'It's tomato juice, and it's got Clamato in it which is clams and tomato…and it has got walnuts but it has a bit of vodka in it but you wouldn't know it had any in it…it tastes like fruit juice…it is like a Bloody Mary…oh and there are lots of umbrellas.'

You can imagine, can't you, how much respect every darts player on the planet had for fancy umbrellas in drinks – least of all, the wee Scot.

It also had bloody celery in it.

'Try it,' I urged with no ounce of responsibility for the man's health.

Five hours later, I am beaten in the Quarters and I am out. You can probably guess it is not the kind of drink that takes you very long to down. I wander back over to the bar.

Jocky is still there. I wouldn't like to estimate how many he had sunk but I had played an entire tournament while he had sat at the bar. I left one of the nicest guys in darts in a place he shouldn't really have been but did so with him quite content,

184

tomato juice all around his mouth and a counter full of stupid little umbrellas flicked everywhere.

'These Caesars are fucking good,' is his parting shot.

Then he falls off his chair.

Chapter Twenty-Five

More Room For Two

Reg Harding and I were heading for the World Pairs in Ayr. To the non-darts fan, I am sure it reads that there seem to be a lot of 'world' this and that in some very odd locations! Welcome to our world in fact.

Ayr just about took the biscuit. Everybody was staying in the player's hotel. You made your own way and it was a pig to get to. I took a train up to London and met up with about four or five others. It was going to be a long expensive journey and I always resented paying for food on whatever British Rail was now called, so of course, the professional sportsman made his own sandwiches and tucked them under his arm and boarded the train all the way to Scotland. Beef butties all the way – but no butter. So, I just substituted it for some thick English mustard!

I am not saying that darts players' mentality got above their station with the The Split and TV money. We were still the same down to earth working-class lads. Nobody from Oxbridge was ever gonna light up Blackpool on a Bank Holiday Weekend but when you look back – as is a general idea with an autobiography

– you do laugh at just how tin pot the individual's organisation was whether the *organisation* itself was 'professional' or not.

I was due to hook up with Freddie Williams, the PDC's main caller and Phil Jones the MC – always both great company and obviously, a massive part of the stage management of a day at the darts.

Freddie was starving obviously, and I was the man with the sandwich plan. There was nothing to do on a train trip to Ayr except eat and play cards and Freddie would play anyone anywhere and soon he was chomping at the bit for one of my delicious home-made butties.

'What have you got Shayne?' he asked.

'Do you like a bit of beef and mustard?' I replied.

I should have really answered mustard and beef.

Chomping at the bit soon became vomiting from the hip. He took one bite and all the colours of the rainbow flashed before me in an instant. He is coughing and spluttering everywhere. I thought he was having a coronary.

Naturally, he wouldn't touch my contributions after that but did live to tell to the tale. Not forever though, he has departed us since as we now begin that roll call of those who have left both the darts world and this world and from this point on, I should warn you that death is a theme. A recurring theme, like Australian Tony's recurring dream.

Tony knew he was going to win and I started to see people

around me kicking the bucket. You looked at Jocky and you looked in the mirror. I think it went with the territory and I am pretty sure that in my lifetime nothing will change. Darts was the one sport where it really didn't matter what your body mass index was so long as you could fit into the Hawaiian shirt. If you happen to think chess is a sport, I will allow you in our unique category too.

The evidence was all there. This game was not lifestyle conducive. Only mental fitness counted and your physical prowess would call time on you at some point.

We get to Ayr. No excitement in this game at arriving at a new venue. No cultural involvement from any of the players. The biggest misunderstanding between 'professional' sports players and the public is that all this travel is glitz and glamour. I can tell you it is public transport, hotel rooms and performance.

You don't see places at all but I can inform you that I have seen enough of Ayr to tell you it has not yet emerged from the 1960s. Include in that, the hotel rooms which a heavy-handed Reg was intent on destroying. Off came the knobs from the TV and the ironing board was destroyed in an instant. He was not aggressive just bloody clumsy and it made a shithole of a hotel worse in an instant. Reg too was starving and took the last of my reject sausage rolls knowing that it was off.

You will eat anything when you have to endure the British rail network all the way to Scotland. The next thing – Reg is moaning he is feeling a bit dickey. Then he tells me a few people are moaning about a bug. I remind him that he should have declined the sausage roll and taken my sandwich instead as Freddie had unwisely done!

That was a good point for him to spew up everywhere. Then, develop the shits. From that moment on, he was in and out of the bog every ten minutes. I bought him soup to settle the stomach but there was no calming that tsunami down. Everything was flying out of him. He was farting so much that the duvet was levitating.

'Does it stink in here?' he asked politely and weakly. 'It must.'

No Reg, it's OK,' I lied.

As I opened the room door, I spied the maid spraying air freshener everywhere. It was that bad, it had spread everywhere.

I had to leave. There is no way I was staying in that shit-stained shit hotel and God, I dreaded returning to it. So, I went for a curry and bumped into Eric. There was only one way to get the shits. The steaming hot, natural way! Bristow loved a hot curry but my goodness me, he could eat at temperatures the rest of us couldn't dream of touching. I could feel Vindaloo coming off his order and he ate it all in one go without the blink of an eye. I was struggling and bagged up the leftovers, thinking I would eat it all tomorrow.

When I got back to the room, Reg was calming down but one

thing the darts tour has taught me over the years is that there is a massive difference between when you think you are ready and the reality. Burgess-induced food poisoning or not, it has to be the worst sport in the world for nutrition. You eat shit, you drink shit and it Reg's case do nothing but shit shit – and it doesn't really matter when you are due on, you somehow get the brain in gear even when your arse is literally bringing up the rear.

We had all got used to the lifestyle that if Reg was feeling that he could now eat and wanted the leftovers of my curry, then I would not stand in his way.

My vindaloo lay floating in a basin of hot water to warm it up.

Then the next morning, I am sat in the bog demolishing those very leftovers. Reg is banging on the toilet door. I am tucking into a tasty Indian breakfast! Fat people do this. Darts players do this. Reg is hammering that door down.

I let him in. That sausage roll has killed him. I would imagine there can't be many better ways to wake up to the smell of a leftover Indian and a whiff of a poorly tummy.

I don't even remember how that tournament panned out. I have just googled it – such are the beauties of writing an autobiography that you can't even embellish the truth any more which was a standard feature of the darts world. It seems I crashed and burned. The longest trip on the planet to Scotland with everyone else's arse on fire. The truth was the opposite when

190

it came to the darts. Nobody lit up the tournament.

All I know is that revenge is sweet and that on the way home, Reg got his by the boatload. By the way, there is no comparison between the journey and anticipation (even if nervous or out of form) of heading to an event and the trip back (even if you have won). The going to is always much better than the going from.

I bombed out of the tournament and spent the entire journey home on the disabled bog. That is a long way to be incapacitated. I literally did not come for air…all the way back from Ayr.

In the early 1990s I was rooming at the Ramada Inn, Kensington with Ian Carpenter at the British Open – and playing Pairs with him. Pairs days took place before the Singles.

I got talking to a pretty decent player from Norfolk by the name of Phil Gilman whom I had known for years – a real larger than life character. Funny how we say that a lot about darts players. The nature of the sport – drinking pints, having a nickname, turning to the crowd and giving it some meant that it was a title that was readily available to all of us.

The truth is that Phil and I just connected. We were on the same wavelength. We could have been separated at birth. Suddenly the subject of eating game came up! He hadn't had any rabbit for years.

'I've got a load of rabbit in my bag,' I announced. 'I've fried it up in onions and bacon.'

Well sod the darts. I can't tell you how good this sounded

against the monotony of over-priced and over-cooked hotel food.

'You've got rabbit in your room?' He was salivating at the mouth.

Not only did we think the same, we ate the same.

'Yeah, bread and butter too,' I added as if it were some rare delicacy.

We were pretty simple folk.

'I've gotta come to your room,' he invited himself.

Sure enough – three or four little bunnies were waiting for us and we chewed on them like vultures who had not eaten for weeks. We were in heaven. But realistically one step up from being a tramp. Like all good tramps, I hadn't intended to share my banquet but we were – dare I say it – rabbiting on all night in the throes of one of the greatest spontaneous drinking sessions on the circuit.

And then guess who won the bloody British Open that year? Phil 'The Bunny' Gilman. No, that wasn't his nickname but it obviously did him good.

He ate the game then fucking won it!

This was not an isolated incident and further proof that the body clock of the body of a darts player is just 24/7. We will eat anything and everything at any hour of the day. So many matches went late into the night it was impossible not to balloon. Self-discipline obviously didn't exist either!

Reg too took to rabbit. He was staying with my first wife

Andrea and I on the eve of the Eastbourne Open. Obviously, I have not really mentioned the missus much but I think you are aware that multiple darts players had multiples wives – such was the lifestyle.

I awoke at 4 a.m, which was not unusual.

'I'm gonna get rabbit for breakfast,' I announced though I don't think anyone took a blind bit of notice.

Why would you? It was clearly the only time in their life that they had heard such a ridiculous statement.

So, I got up and out and went round all my local hot spots where I knew I could find one at this time of the morning. It would have been impossible during the day of course. But I caught nothing. I couldn't get a bunny for love nor money.

I had to give up. No rabbit for breakfast. I never failed like this before.

I am on the way back, dejected about from a mile from home. What happens? Slam. Straight into a rabbit. Literally caught in the headlights. Well, I had no choice, did I? I had flattened the front of it completely. All I could salvage were the back legs so cleaned the thing up, skinned it and got to preparing a back leg each complete with bacon and beans. Nobody complained. Housemate happy. The bunny hit my reg. Reg found my bunny a hit.

On that note the publisher has just called by the way asking if I have remembered the brief to aim this book at the vegetarian market. Can't get much of a signal these days in certain parts of Hastings…

Chapter Twenty-Six

Auf Wiedersehen Pet!

The German market had now opened up for me. This was perfect campervan territory. I was starting to pick up some exhibition work and if you were slipping down the rankings and suffering self-doubt about your overall ability then a trip to Deutschland was just what the doctor ordered. A Welsh chap called Louis Kirkup called.

He and a few of his mates were erecting electricity pylons across what was the old East Germany. This was proper stereotypical British labourer abroad mentality. Dirty gritty labour in the heat. Bags of cash. Beer by night. Shag the local girls. All of them. Even those with a tache. Would I head out to Remptendorf and do some gigs? What on earth would give you the impression that I would say yes?!

Well, the first time I actually flew out but I knew instantly it was time to get the van wheels back out on the roads. I mention it to my mate and lodger Fred Frewin who said he would come for the ride. That is the last time I will honour Fred with his full name. He is of course the legendary Fred The Spread.

Can you imagine a cemetery for darts players? Not a proper name in sight and not enough room on the headstone to put all those bloody nicknames. I only mention this because everyone in this book dies on me at some point.

And Fred was an ex-international boxer and an accomplished super league darts player. But, In fact he was actually a plasterer – hence the nickname.

Anyway, Fred The Spread thought this sounded like an adventure – and who wouldn't think that…so we packed up, hit the cross channel ferry, made a mental note not to buy fags and headed for Brussels.

No better place to break down is there than the Brussels Ring Road. Conk conk conk. The van grinds to a halt with half of Belgium watching.

I have no choice but to ring the AA, knowing that we will probably be here for hours. Then, the bombshell.

'You didn't book European Cover, Sir.'

SHIT.

'Can I have a number for a local garage?' I plead.

'No, fuck off, you thick cunt.' Was not the exact phrase the telephonist responded with but it might as well have been.

Shit. We are stuck. Absolutely stranded.

I decide to ring Louis pathetically:

'I know you are in Germany, but can you help?'

We were in a totally different era of mobile phones – in terms of technology and cost. This was great – stranded and racking up bills before we had earned a penny.

Louis says he will see what he can do.

It was better than the AA's response but doesn't fill me with confidence and nor does it alter the fact that every flipping car in Belgium is flying past me while we are trying to get heard and stay safe.

About an hour later, Louis calls back and gives me a number of a bloke who will help. Somebody always knew somebody who knew somebody! So, I thought I would give it a go. Actually, I had no fucking choice but to ring and I get a bloke who answers in Dutch.

'You speak English?'

I start doing that thing we do by raising the volume and putting large gaps in between my words when you think you are talking to a foreigner.

'Yesh, yesh,' he replied like a stereotypical Dutchman.

'I need assistance,' I told him.

There was no other way of putting it.

'Give me your co-ordinates,' he replied.

I didn't have a clue where he was – or really where I was.

'I am on the Brussels Ring Road…Junction 14 …the E35.' I hope that makes sense.

Then, nothing.

'I don't understand,' he broke the silence. 'Where are you?'

'I'm in …fucking…Brussels…' I shout.

'I need your co-ordinates,' he replied with military precision.

'What fucking co-ordinates,' I shout. 'I am in Brussels on the Ring Road.'

Then all I hear is a sniggering laughter and I am starting to lose it big time, shouting against the traffic:

'Don't fucking laugh at me.'

Then more silence.

'I am sorry, I don't mean to laugh.' But you could hear him smiling.

'I'm a tug boat in the North Sea.'

I didn't think he had a long enough rope to get me off the Ring Road. But I wasn't about to ask either. To this day, I have no idea where Louis got the number from for a tug boat in the North Sea.

I have no choice but to set off on foot. Through a hedge, I spot a Doctor's surgery. They will know. They are in the emergency services game so they by nature will have numbers and offer to help. My logic was amazing, wasn't it?

I don't even know how we managed to communicate. The girls in the surgery called their boyfriends one by one. This was a farce. To my astonishment a car turned up. Fifteen minutes later, this Belgian bloke is popping up my bonnet and I am feeling like the biggest numpty in Europe.

'Have you got an immobiliser fitted?' he asked.

It was amazing how when we are so shit at speaking foreign languages then anyone on the continent can just start using car speak in English.

'Yeah, two years ago,' I told him.

Next thing. He rips a fucking wire out.

'Try the ignition,' he gesticulated.

Va va voom. We were in business. I felt a prick. Completely mortified in front of Fred The Spread, my roadside mechanic and of course everybody in Belgium who drove past me that day. I know I am just one of millions of people who has sat by the side of a road, sweating and thinking you will never get out of here only to be merrily back in your car a few moments later wondering why you ever worried.

My Belgian friend didn't accept a penny. That is why I love Belgians. We drove off the five or six hours towards Germany. I am sure he went back to his little café-tabac that night laughing about how fucking stupid ze English are and let's face it, us English do the same, don't we? One unfortunate moment is enough to tar an entire nation with the same brush. So, on behalf of everybody in England, I apologise for bringing our country into disrepute and being the only person ever to break down abroad!

As for the twat in the tugboat – and I won't even get started on how Louis thought he was the man with the plan – well, I look forward to you getting stuck in the ocean and somebody giving you my number.

By the time we arrived, it was about 8 or 9 at night and there was only one thing to do. We went straight on the piss. So knackered were we that I am sure we were half cut after the first one!

We ended up at Louis's place with Fred on the floor on a single mattress. By 3 a.m I awoke to find it was minus 20 and chucking it down with snow. I will give the morning rabbit run a miss, eh.

I am half asleep and half cut when it dawns on me that there is a constant knocking at the front door. Everybody is asleep and I don't really want to answer it. It's not my house after all. I've only been here a couple of hours.

I open the door. It's Fred in his pants.

'What the fuck are you doing there?' I ask disorientated.

'I was trying to find the bog and ended up going out the front door …' His teeth chatter as he tries to respond.

He is blue.

I am still too pissed to ask why he had even managed to get outside.

'How long you been there?' I quiz him.

I hadn't even let him in at this point.

'About 20 minutes,' he guesses.

Geez. He was a state. If I hadn't woken up, it is safe to say that Fred The Spread would be Fred The Dead. He wasn't even warm by morning and the next day the darts began.

The exhibitions went down a storm – this was my bread and butter really and I had done it so many times. Turn up, show off, have banter, get pissed in a place where there wasn't much going on in the way of entertainment. *Be* that entertainment.

Louis was happy with everything and with just 48 hours or so before we were due to head back home, gave us a day off and told us about this soft tip tournament just a little down the road. So, we thought 'easy pickings and why not?'

So, I approach the organiser and tell him I would like to pay my money to enter.

'No, no,' he protested. 'I know who you are. You're not playing. People here are threatening not to play if you are allowed to.'

The village hall was seething with unrest!

'I don't play soft tip,' I protested. 'I only play steel tip.'

'No, no…' The organiser was unnecessarily shitting his pants.

We reached a compromise:

'If you stay, will you present the prizes as a professional?' He suddenly saw an opportunity.

'Well, I ain't gonna do it for nothing,' I replied. 'Chuck in a couple of beers and you have a deal.'

Then I spied this big hamper of German sausages on the table.

'I want them sausages too,' I demanded.

'OK, OK,' he caved in.

Negotiation was not his strong point.

'That's a good spread, Fred,' I said to Fred The Spread.

Who was not dead.

Once we're in, I am not really paying any attention to the darts during the day. I am just trying to have a laugh and a few drinks. Plus, I can't make out any of the announcements. German was not my strong point. Come to think of it, nor was my English.

Suddenly, the guy on the mic is announcing the Top Three and I haven't got a clue what is going on except for a presentation ceremony looks the same in any language albeit the quality of the prizes varies.

I am needed at the front urgently. The organiser hands me a fridge magnet.

'What the fuck is this?' I ask politely!

'That's his prize for third place,' I am told. 'This is not a big tournament'.

No kidding. Don't tell me anyone is getting a chicken dinner here, please.

They announce second place. By a process of elimination rather than instantaneous translation, I manage to conclude this.

The runner-up approaches the organiser who whispers something in his ear. Then he looks at me like a piece of shit. He is giving me the eyes as though he is going to stab me. He refuses to shake my hand and walks off.

'What was that about?' I turn to the man with the clipboard.

'He won the sausages but I gave them to you,' he replies nervously.

Then it dawns on me:

'You gave me the runner's up prizes?' I question him.

Admittedly, I had asked for them.

'I'll sort it,' he wobbles, scared like a mouse that it is all going to kick off as he had feared when allowing me to register. I had ruined everyone's fun!

Then the winner emerges.

I am slightly embarrassed.

I am about to demand a trade for cobbled together selection of second rate second prize meats.

They pass me the prize to award to the champ.

Well, congratulations, Mein Herr.

I had to hand to him. And I had to hand it to him too.

That was well worth an afternoon of darts.

The meat didn't look so bad now.

After all, I didn't really want to be driving home with first prize of an electric bench grinder in the back of the van!

Jesus. What the hell was all that about? That was what he won.

The winner seemed happy. I can't say I was not embarrassed for the guy nor the sport of darts. Hey, this was a game where you got a meal and fifteen quid for representing your country. That piece of kit was definitely worth more.

Maybe I come from a professional sportsman's mentality and perhaps these little villagers were just happy to play darts and win *something* but I couldn't quite work out how an electric bench grinder was an appropriate prize for a darts tournament.

They even held a village festival while we were there which was an all-day event where someone would pretend to be vicar ordained for 24 hours and you had the right to marry any girl you wanted for ten minutes and take her behind a curtain and do whatever you wanted to do. It was up to you in that democratic, sexist way that the local law allowed.

I can tell you that on the day of the festival all the good-looking girls had left town! And after a bellyful of food you really didn't fancy the leftovers.

Either way, I knew from vast experience when it was time to leave as Herman The German was eyeing me up. This really was small town Eastern Europe in a modern Germany where many of the mentalities of Soviet restriction seemed to linger despite unification. Parochialism was king.

Heading back home, I started on the hamper, taking a bite out of one of the sausages. And one bite was all I took. I wound down the window and chucked the lot out – the hamper and all its food. Of course, by the time I got to taste my winnings it had been sat out all day on a table with no refrigeration and sweaty Germans palms brushing past it.

All that for a game of darts…on my day off from darts…with a fridge magnet for the guy who comes third, a grinder for the winner and a fight over the reward for second place even though as prizes go, it was the wurst.

Chapter Twenty-Seven

In Van-ness

Three lessons from Germany. Check the fucking van before travel. Life on the road is crazy. But remember, at all times, play darts. When that started to slip, the good times would not be there any more. No fancy trips with free beer and shitty sausages. Always remember you are a darts player first and a tourist second.

I can say that now but I didn't take a blind bit of notice of myself, of course.

Also – don't make any more sausage puns. You have done the wurst one twice now.

Next stop Inverness…a mere 16 hours in the van straight in one go from Hastings! And the longest road ever to nowhere. You get to the A9 and you think you are nearly there and you've still got hours to drive. Predictably, this was not the preparation of a professional sportsman and by the time I got there I was too fucking knackered to play. I played absolute shit and was dumped out in the first round. *Out* in the first round. A waste of time and petrol. I had over done it. The only pleasure was that I did shoot one rabbit.

I think I might have spotted that tug in the North Sea too.

Word spreads like flies at tournaments – whether it be Burgess being bent for throwing a match or talk of The Split back in the day, the internal communication of the pro darts player is literally Chinese Whispers and you turn your life around on a whim. All those tournaments in the States, we just hit the road and turned up.

Now, I was hearing that there was a tournament on in Blackpool on just about the way home. I had nothing to lose as I had already done that so thought I would chance my arm and with just £50 in my pocket, pulled out of Inverness more or less as quickly as I had arrived and made for Fort William, Loch Ness, Glasgow and I wasn't even half way there by this point.

I filled the van up with enough to get me home. I now have just £15 left. I know what you are thinking. I needed a win. Too right, I did. At least I had no hotel bills to pay for. Equally, I knew I was one van breakdown away from financial disaster.

By the time I made it to the seaside, I just parked up in some god-forsaken dump of a street and abandoned it to walk into town. The phrase stretch your legs never applied more after 16 hours up to Scotland and then almost straight back.

By fluke, or maybe I always did this, I ended up talking to some bloke in a pub. He said he recognised me and introduced himself as Kevin Reaney. He owned the nearby hotel The

Lexham.

I began to tell him my story of how disastrous the trip to Inverness had been and that on a chance like that which had failed, I was now broke. I told him I had parked up miles away.

'I own some flats.' Kev came to the rescue. 'You can park outside on the pavement and you won't get a ticket. No problem, at all.'

Short term issue resolved but it didn't escape that my darts were slipping away and so was any money I was making. It takes a lot to keep getting yourself up for long journeys and little reward when players you never used to fear were now claiming your scalp.

Kevin introduced me to his wife Carol and I got to know them well over the years. They were both very kind towards me and would come to watch me play and even though I had only just met them. I was feeling the loneliness of the van whereas I had always seen that emotion as the *freedom* of the van. That space and gypsy-like lifestyle which I had loved was now suffocating me as there was more going out than going in.

By the time, I had paid my tenner to enter the tournament at The Winter Gardens, I literally had enough money for about a pint and a half and I certainly was not in a position to offer Kevin anything back.

I stooped to a new low. I am ashamed to say that I would wait until I saw people leaving and take the dregs of their leftover beer trying to make up a whole pint from their remains.

Pitiful, I know. You may well think that it is darts and it was always going to end this way and that's fair enough. Getting this far in the book has provided me with so many great memories of stuff I had largely parked in the memory bank but obviously when I read that back, I realise it is embarrassing and desperate.

But that is where I was.

Thankfully, I *was* playing brilliantly. I had no choice. I don't know if that desperation on this occasion gave me an edge. It is hard to say because I had been close to this situation before but I think the futility of the trip to Inverness and the length of the journey really underlined it this time. Talking to Kev and seeing through his kindness that there was some good in the world definitely helped but equally you can't put that pressure on yourself that it is shit or bust when you enter a tournament. You just have to throw the darts.

As with so often in the past, I did not have a plan B if Blackpool didn't come off. Thankfully, I took Alan The Iceman Warriner out in the final and scooped £500.

I can't tell you what that meant to me in terms of confidence and cash. Let's put it in layman terms. At today's rates it is the equivalent of about 25 electric bench grinders. The Iceman was out in the cold even in The Winter Gardens.

Just like celebrating in the States with the enormous bottle of Jack Daniels, the temptation was to re-fuel yourself with a treat even though you knew you needed the money longer term. It was human nature of course but the stark truth is that if you won you spent it and headed back towards debt. If you lost, well…you were there anyway.

I asked Kev if I could have a room for a night at the hotel. In fact, I stayed for two and he never charged me. I am extremely grateful for his friendship. He was just a fan who became a friend. The reality is that he knew my CV inside out – even the tobacco run stories. How did he find that out?!

But you can't stay forever and darts shows you that these are just moments in time so after hanging on for 48 hours after my victory, it was time to say goodbye and head down the M6 and make the still very long journey home.

I am halfway home when I begin to think something is not right. It starts to smell… really stink …a putrid whiff. Well, it wasn't Jamie Bravefart. He wasn't on this trip. I had no idea where it was coming from except it was in my van that I hardly driven for three days so God knows how long it has been in there. And it got steadily worse.

I always kept it tidy and a big curtain separated the cab from the back so I could actually feel like it was a home and not a car but eventually I said to myself that next time I see a sign for Services then I would pull over and take a look.

So, I opened up the back at the next available moment and I could not believe my eyes. I couldn't see the floor at all. While I was in The Lexham, thousands of maggots had moved in here. Squatters rights.

That rabbit I shot in Inverness…I left the bones in the back, didn't I? The publisher will ring in a minute and remind me about the veggies again. The flies had gone for the remains and the maggots had taken residence. Everybody was looking at me asking what the hell was I doing and what was going on in the back of my van. I needed to get out of there fast.

I couldn't stay, but nor could I drive home with that stench. It was the most vile sight of my life. I didn't have the equipment nor the front to clean it at the Services so that left me with no choice. And there was still such a long way to go plus when I got home there was no way I was going to do anything except crash so that meant they had another night to wreck the joint.

The following day, I took the world's biggest bucket of bleach and started work. It was a thankless task. Serves you right – the vegetarians fight back. Fair enough. When I was finally content that it was habitable again but not really sure if I would ever view it in the same light, I went back to the van a couple of days later and discovered there were now about 10 million blue bottles. Now, I had to get the floorboards up and get under them and clean all over again.

The following morning, I went back to the scene of the crime. The same again. There they were fucking with my head on behalf of all rabbits everywhere. They had re-hatched. The whole process lasted a week before I was in the clear. I can't believe that such little pesky irritants had such a hold over me.

I am sure – vegetarian or not – that you are delighted to hear that I would never leave the remains of an animal in my van ever again, and with my decline in form leaving me teetering financially in a rollercoaster existence of highs and lows from near bankruptcy to short term cash injections, it was not just a rabbit that I had to pick the bones out of.

Chapter Twenty-Eight

All Is Quiet On New Year's Day

I hadn't quite given up on the van yet even though the clues were all there. It was giving up on me sooner rather than later. It certainly didn't have many more trips to Scotland left in it and I couldn't afford to keep the Bleach industry going single-handedly.

I just about limped to the Circus Tavern in Purfleet near Dagenham for The World Championships. I benefit from the strange affection shown to me of the Peter Stringfellow lookalike owner who took a shine my way and allowed me to park the campervan in the car park – privileges normally reserved for Phil!

This is now the second time the gorgeous well-toned Burgess athlete has been hit on by a member of the same sex. If I had stayed around long enough in that little village in Eastern Germany, I believe there were possibilities to expand my horizons there.

All the time the fans are packing the venue and all the TV images going right around the world and whatever you think of the way us darts players built our images with our shirts,

213

nicknames and raucous behaviour, who knew that we were living in the venue car park!

I am due on at 2 p.m New Year's Eve. You can imagine that the party starts early for that day's crowd! After the game, I retire to the van. New Year is really not my scene especially after what happened to Woody and I am more than happy to get back and watch TV.

I must have seen a couple of hours or so of absolute dross, and nodded off. So, unfortunately did the battery. I guess it packed up about two in the morning. Well, in the early hours of New Year, you think 'no bother'. Someone will give me a jump in the morning.

I awake on New Year's Day. To a ghost town. There is an eight-foot wired fence all around me. The car park is deserted. There is no darts for another 24 hours. Not a soul in sight. Everybody has gone.

I try to start the van, knowing it won't. I have no heating. No light. No TV. No battery. And worse, no phone. I am absolutely fucked.

I am freezing, cocooned in the van wearing everything I can possibly find. It is the first time I have worn two woolly hats. I am out of options. There is nothing I can do. I have to wait it out. I lie down. I get up. I walk around the car park kicking my heels thinking someone will come soon. Nobody comes at all. I tell myself that there is nothing to do except go back to bed even though I am freezing. Then I convince myself that I must stay awake at all costs just on the off chance that somebody comes along. How stupid am I? How did I not hear everyone leave this morning? Why didn't the fake Stringfellow tell me that this was the likely scenario? Oh, for fuck's sake. Happy New Year!

There was no play on New Year's Day back then either to allow everyone to see their families so I really was totally up shit creek without a paddle.

I had no choice but to bed down for the night and hope I didn't freeze to death.

On 2 January at 11 a.m, I hear the burly sound of Mr Jobsworth with all his keys bustling around in the car park. I had waited nearly somewhere around the 36-hour mark before I could even think about going anywhere and even then I still had to look for someone to give me a jump start.

Of all the lock-ins that I had witnessed whilst playing and all the blind eyes that were turned, now I had been on the other end of it – except this time they really had shut me in …and thrown away the key.

Chapter Twenty-Nine

After The Horse Has Bolted

The legend and myself had crossed paths a fair few times over the years. It was inevitable. He lived in Lewes, just down the road from Hastings. Despite my migration to the Kent leagues, if you were any good, you all knew each other round these parts.

I had seen him win the Jersey Open and The Courage Best of the Best, as a London County player knew he was quite highly regarded. People often talk about natural ability.

Reg Harding was the most gifted player I ever saw.

He could hit anything on a dartboard. He was made for showing off at exhibitions. Part of his repertoire included using fence nails and fondue sticks.

The ice was broken at The British Open back at The Ramada Inn when I found out he was sleeping in his Citroen in the underground car park to save money. So, it wasn't just me then. It was a ridiculous way to manage professional sport. I was in the hotel and he knocked on the door to ask if he could use my shower. From that moment on, we became really good mates.

Not like that!

I began to get used to the sight of Reg eating.

We soon realised why Reg was known as 'The Horse'…because he fucking ate like one.

Reg, myself and Ian 'Chippy' Carpenter were due to go for a curry. Ian popped back to his room for a few moments. When he didn't instantly re-appear Reg 'The Horse' Harding was not about to wait furlong.

With a Belgian bun in his mouth, we made for the nearest sit down cod and chips. Chippy Carpenter was nowhere to be seen. Chippy Tea was being demolished.

Large cod, buttered rolls – and obviously a portion of ribs. Reg was yet to pick his main course!

Well fed – or so I thought – we made our way back to the hotel.

We bump into Ian Carpenter:

'I've been fucking looking for you everywhere,' he moaned. 'I'm starving where the hell have you been.

'We've been for a chippy, Chippy,' Reg replied.

'I thought we were going for a curry,' he pleaded like a man who hadn't eaten for weeks.

'No problem,' The Horse grunted back. 'I'll go for a curry and chips with you if you want.'

The horse was not about to bolt.

'You can't eat a curry after cod and chips,' fat man Burgess protested.

I felt green at the thought of it.

'Watch me,' the prize stallion responded.

Actually, he was built like a brick shithouse – whatever one of those is.

And he proceeded to demolish a curry in a hurry, eight popadums and naan bread. I couldn't eat a thing. We were left open-mouthed at where he was putting it. His gob wasn't open long enough.

I obviously was drawn to a man who could eat but old Reg could put it away better than anyone. Stuff as simple as this draws you to people on the circuit. A chance conversation can lead to a lifetime of discovery. So we started playing Pairs together.

I wasn't the only one who could see his immense talent. Phil Taylor would quite often grab him to practise against at tournaments. He was like the pacemaker in a long-distance race. Rarely known for his own ability but yet players wanted to be in his company to better themselves and if Phil Taylor was pulling you aside to warm up with, then that is how good he really was. Even in his twilight years, he still had it.

It begs the question – what did he lack that stopped him being a great himself? I think he often didn't get the rub of the green and yes – I know you can't blame bad luck over the course of a career because it does tend to even itself out – but he was more than happy and would often come back laughing after taking $15 off Phil in a practise without batting an eyelid even if

The Power then won 50K the same day. He just didn't have that killer instinct to take titles relentlessly. Play him for a burger in a pub and he would rip shreds off you.

I can't put my finger on how Reg worked. He was the best but his track record denies this. It is naïve to say that anyone was in this just for the fun of it and that he didn't enjoy the whole razzmatazz of the circuit. But he didn't quite have that x-factor to be a world class professional. That is not say that he was unprofessional and it is to stress that he had more talent than anyone I ever faced, and if you think about people like John Virgo in snooker, he was never one of the stars of the game for winning tournaments but he was *the* star for trick shots and made a TV career out of it. He was the king of the exhibition and to be able pull off illusions and magic like that implies a higher level of skill than someone who can relentlessly pot balls or finish whatever is needed on a darts board. That was Reg – if you like, more interested in the individual nuance of the situation rather than the bigger picture. But, he was as good as Jimmy White who lost in the odd World Championship Final in the snooker but somehow did not have that finishing touch to get over the line.

Maybe he failed to understand why Phil wanted to practise against him and then would walk off with the cash and the trophy the next day. Probably – he did not believe or know how good he truly was.

As a pair, we were somewhere between the Chuckle Brothers

219

and Dumb and Dumber. American Customs were sick the sight of us. They were always pulling us. Often, we would turn up with shaved heads and were attempting to enter the country on a tourist visa and would try to pull the wool over their eyes with just a travel bag in our hand luggage. I confess, we did look dodgy.

They would always give us the third degree at Chicago's O Hare or Boston's Logan Airport. We made out we were just over for a laugh but if we had said we were playing for money they would have thrown us straight in a room for 24 hours. If we told them we were 'collecting points' on the circuit, they would just wish us good luck and wave us through. Nuts, really – on both sides! I mean we were the only people going transatlantic with just hand luggage! Before 9/11 – ridiculously, I know – we would walk on with our darts. After September 11th, you couldn't even joke about it. Obviously, I understand why but frankly, I don't look like one of Bin Laden's disciples, do I?

But it was always a laugh and I associate many of the best memories with Reg – because he was such a top player but also because of the quality of the scrape we would get into. On one occasion, we flew into Montreal, Canada with Paul Butler, Dennis 'Breezer Geezer' Smith and Mark 'Tommo' Thomson and decided to hire a 7-seater to drive through Winnipeg and on to Saskatoon.

Nobody was asking the key question. Where was Butler's

nickname?

Paul and I were sharing the driving. Reg, Mark and Dennis were playing cards – for about 3000 bloody miles. Reg kept losing, copping the hump and throwing the lot out the window, making me stop at every service station to buy another pack as though somehow, he was playing with a cursed deck! He would lose again and out the window they would go in a fit of rage and I would have to pull over half an hour later for a fresh set.

If only Reg had that ethic and angst about the darts which he almost saw as a bit of a fun even though he had a real crack at making a living at it. The cards drove him potty though.

That was nothing. I am listening to all this banter and nonsense coming from the back and not really concentrating on negotiating the woodland you get out in these parts when I spot a massive moose beyond the trees. I am yelling at the guys to put down the cards and take a look and of course, as always happens when you are pointing stuff out, you don't see what is in front of you. What was right before me? A baby bear runs in front of the car and I am split seconds from a head-on. I veer slightly off the road trying to avoid it and take a slice out of the number plate.

Damn, that beats a hare and a rabbit every day of the week. I almost had him too. And if I had, his Mum would have come for us, I am sure. Car reg damaged this time. Reg in car unmoved.

Like all flawed geniuses, Reg had his troubles – funds being the least of them. When your health goes, the money is almost irrelevant. We were due to travel to Bochum in Germany for the German Open. The plan was to drive.

Obviously crossing the channel and getting there in one place – based on previous experience – was not going to be plain sailing. So, to speak.

Reg's health had taken a turn and had to have a catheter fitted. He was still playing to a very high standard. In fact, he was routinely (and ironically) taking the piss out of perceived better players. We were due to leave in my little Ford Fiesta Van. Predictably, the cam belt snapped on it a couple of days beforehand! The only surprising thing about that is that it didn't wait until we were heading up the ramp on to the cross-channel ferry. I really did miss talking to the man in the North Sea.

I needed Reg to magic something out of thin air. He had about four Renault 7s outside his house which he was supposed to be doing up. They were all worth about £50 – scrap! I told him straight – we can't get to Germany; my car is fucked.

'But none of them are runners,' he protested unsurprisingly.

'I need you to come up with a car Reg or Germany's out.'

That's a car, Reg…not a car reg.

My bags were packed for the Friday.

Friday comes and Reg calls to say he has come up trumps. He pulls up outside the house in an Austin Maestro 1.3 1989 automatic. Geez – when this car came out, the Berlin Wall was still standing. I soon learned the truth. It *had* cost £50. He bought it off his neighbour.

It gets better. It had also failed its MOT, needed welding and we were about to drive to Germany in it. I knew this was unlikely to get to Bochum and back. I didn't ever bother checking for European Cover this time. One thing was certain – this trip was going to come crashing down on us much quicker than anything that happened in Berlin in 1989.

We had no choice but to try to set off. I wasn't even certain we would make the next county let alone the next country.

So off we set and I am giving it full throttle. After a few minutes I am thinking 'well, so far so good' then I am heading through France and starting to think it is going like a dream. This, of course, is too good to be true.

I am dreading Belgium because of past experience of course…I equally laugh to myself and shit myself at the prospect of breaking down at exactly the same place and the same guy coming out.

Everything is going too well.

We stop for petrol. I know, you don't really want to stop this thing for the fear of it never starting again.

Reg is hesitant.

'Come on,' I urge. 'Let's get going.'

'No,' he placed his hand on the dash. 'You have to wait until it's cool.'

Now, he tells me.

'The fuel line is too close to the manifold. When the engine is off, the fuel evaporates,' he announces. 'Once the engine is cool, the fuel will get through again.'

For fuck's sake. If you really want the thing to cool down, let me book a week in for travel next time.

We push the car to the corner. We wait 20 minutes. It starts. Do I have to wait 20 minutes every bloody time we stop? Apparently so. Oh, I can hardly wait for the next truckstop. 20 minutes in a German layby. Does it get any better than this? Right up there will all those maggots in Chorley…and I am not referring to the people in that Lancashire town!

But, I have reduced my expectations from not getting there at all to getting there in stop-starts. I would deal with getting home once I had picked up my electric bench grinder, *off* meat and married the ugliest village virgin for ten minutes.

We arrived so late unfortunately I didn't have time to meet Helga that night, let alone show her my slightly rancid sausage. The next day was the German Open.

Location – oh my God it was take two of that visit to East Germany just on a bigger scale. The German Open is taking place in a school hall. There are 600 blokes in the 'room'. I get to play just one German in the First Round whom I take out with a 161 finish.

A couple of hours later, I am watching Reg versus Eric Claris. Eric doesn't play any more after falling off a ladder and badly injuring his arm. Unlike many of my friends, he is still alive. He went under the name of The Sheriff.

If you are thinking that darts has run out of nicknames at this point, well the truth is that Eric was based just outside of Los Angeles a few years before. He was also massive friends with Eric Clapton.

One day, he was so enraged by the local law enforcement agency after being stopped on the way home from a late-night darts meet. Things got out of hand and he actually took the local Sheriff out with a pistol he kept to ward off unwanted fans. His deputy saved his boss from a near certain death and Eric walked free in a case of mistaken identity. He shot the sheriff but he didn't shoot the deputy.

Clapton wrote the song in memory of the story and Claris assumed the nickname of The Sheriff.

True story.

Is it bollocks? I made the whole thing up – I don't know why he was called The Sheriff at all but I do know that I just re-read that bit back and thought that it was a scenario that seemed more than likely on *my* travels.

He *was* in fact Belgium's Number One at the time. Reg and him were having a right ding-dong.

The Sheriff had taken a big shot in the deciding leg and left a double. Reg The Catheter Harding needed 156. A piece of piss.

Reg's face turns serene. His eyes glaze over.

He steps up.

Treble 20. Treble 20. Double 18. Boom.

I am ecstatic for him.

'Fantastic, brilliant job, Reg.' I punch the air.

His response equals the best I have ever heard.

'I was having a slash when I hit that.'

Reg really did have the deciding leg.

What a line – and proof once again that like no other sport you could be pissed up through booze, on the breadline broke or severely handicapped because they were the cards you were dealt, darts players managed to achieve a focus that lifted them from all the shit going on.

He didn't win the tournament that day. Unfortunately, he lost to some upstart called Burgess but I think you get a sense of the fact that these events come so thick and fast that is only really *the* World Championships that counts. It is the bits in between the tournaments that people remember!

Modesty prevents me from telling you who walked away with the electric bench grinder but I beat Alex 'The Ace of *Herts*' Roy, Mervyn 'The King' King and then 'Diamond' Dave Askew in the final to round off a brilliant trip with The Bulldog crowned German Open champion 2000 which left only one concern.

How the fuck were we getting home? Limping all the way was the answer. Stop, start and 20-minute lay-by breaks. You can see how you might fall out of love with the sport when it is so bloody difficult to get there.

The German trips were exceptional for their randomness. You really didn't know what kind of village mentality you could walk into and if you would get a chance to add to your range of electrical appliances or collection of virgins...but once you had done one run out there, you did start to look for certain things. All the boys on tour would always make a beeline for the Argentinian steakhouses which were phenomenal in Germany. Odd that, I know – what did you most look forward to about Germany? The Argentinian food.

Fact – they were always full of pissed up British dart players. You are on the beer all day and pretty much starving and knackered. You could guarantee to get fed endlessly. It ticked all the boxes several times over – mostly because you would go there knowing that leaving with a doggy bag was part of the deal and when you are on the road, trying to keep the bills down, you always steal and borrow.

And after every final night at the steakhouse came that dawning inevitability of the journey home. I tell Reg I will drive our £50 motor to the ferry. We are on and off the autobahns through Germany, and halfway through Belgium when the dreaded moment comes. It is time to fill up. Here we go again. Time for a 20-minute break during which Reg announces he is hungry. 'Fucking hungry' in fact.

He is thinking I must have left his doggy bag back in the

room. Schoolboy error. I know exactly what I have done with it. They are under the manifold beneath the engine sizzling and piping hot! Reg is like a kid in a sweet shop when we pull over at the service station for an Argentinian steak sandwich. I am shaking my head in disbelief. But then again, I did shoot rabbit and eat piss-stained steaks in Ireland, and believe me, in the chapters ahead…well, wait until we get to my curry!

Somehow, there was method in Reg's madness and the car made it back to Hastings. I think he knew it would get no further though and he got to work welding before selling it *back* to the neighbour for £200. We had made Germany and Reg had made £150.

We both knew though that travelling in the vehicle again was a risk. The steaks were too high.

Chapter Thirty

White Van Man Is Back

You can tell it was the new era even if you couldn't tell what the new era would bring. Not too long after The Split, I am *invited* to Sky headquarters at Isleworth, Middlesex. There are a few of us and it is all hush hush. Peter Manley, Rod Harrington, Cliff Lazarenko and the legendary commentator Sid Wadell are all told to be there in the morning to do an advert for the World Championships.

This was unchartered territory – not only were we regularly on TV but we were making TV. For some reason, the Creative Director had decided that the trailer would take on a Robin Hood theme so you can probably imagine the conversation as we walk into the dressing room:

'I fucking know who they will pick to be Friar Tuck,' said Manley.

To be fair, I don't think casting this role amongst dart players was a difficult call.

'Don't worry, I'll be Friar Tuck.' I knew my fate.

And so Peter became Robin Hood and Rod Will Scarlet, Cliff

was Little John and Sid was Maid Marion.

Obviously, Sid was not Maid Marion but I had you there for a second. He was actually Alan-a-Dale. What is true is that we were all wearing sandals and codpieces. Well, except for me. I had to wear sandals and a smock. Obviously, this is normal for me at weekends in Hastings but it was first for television!

I learned too that Robin Hood's favourite radio show was The Archers. I will leave that with you.

I think too at that stage, all the gimmicks and investment from the game-changing Sky meant that you would almost do whatever they wanted. Nobody was about to do anything diva-ish and say no because this was the channel that had more cameras, more razzmatazz and more money in every sport it invested in. People take touchline reporters and dressing room cameras as normal now but at some point back in the beginning Sky went with their shopping list and said we will pay this for rights but this is how we are going to do it. Some of us, as viewers and sportsmen, can remember want went before.

So, if they wanted me in a bra and stilletos, then they could have me. We didn't get paid for it but we knew that long term, there would be a return.

So, of course, on a TV set there is a lot of waiting around and that means you go to the loo, coffee machine ...whatever...in your codpiece and sandals.

It also means you go out to the car park.

Suddenly, security burst into the green room and are asking whose campervan is parked out there. One of the big directors is jumping up and down.

'Your vehicle is unbecoming of a car in a corporate car park,' I was told.

They thought the gypsies had rolled into town.

Ironic really given that, most of Sky's trucks dwarfed it. I was left with very little choice but to mince my way out to the car park and try to move the thing in my smock and sandals. They were right though. The van was starting to look decrepit. Even though, I do admit, the new cross-dressing me added some elegance to it. I took note.

I deserved an upgrade and in time I went through a few. But it was always the way to travel and yet you were usually taking a risk, picking up something that could let you down at any point but would also come at a bargain price and give you that freedom you needed.

Buying and selling a van was never straight-forward. It was the kind of transaction where you might only get the partial truth. As I did, previous owners tended to modify the vehicle. That meant little quirks and individual traits normally concealed the full-service history.

Potential buyers and sellers would also pick the worst moments to call. I had recently sold a van and was looking for a new one whilst appearing at The World Matchplay in Blackpool.

The Tournament Director tells me I am on in three minutes. I begin my walk on sequence.

The phone rings. I am halfway to the stage.

It is the guy I sold *my* van to. I have a game of darts to play and I am on the telly.

'Your campervan has just broken down,' he yells at me.

'No mate, *your* campervan just broke down.'

'I gotta go, I am on the telly,' I told him.

And hung up.

I never heard from him again. But that's exactly the point. It is like a bad Chinese Whispers of autotrading and every time someone sells one on, the vans get a little bit less like the original vehicle that left the showroom all those years ago and by the time this poor sod bought it from me, I ended up doing to him what people had done to me and he got it for a song. He soon found out.

I didn't do it deliberately. The price reflected how big a turd it was. But it seemed standard fare.

I found a guy in Dorset selling ex-police vehicles and picked up a Mercedes Sprinter 4800 with a view to converting it into a camper. It was one of the biggest mistakes of my life! It had been a Metropolitan Police meat wagon.

It had four or five seats that needed ripping out and a caged area in the back to lock the old piss heads in but basically ran alright. That was the main thing. Didn't want to end up calling

232

North Sea Emergency Rescue again. It was quite a big van and I took a shine to it. In fact, it seemed perfect.

Don't they all?! I got it home and ripped the whole thing to pieces, selling all its contents on E-Bay. The police had been decent enough to strip the vehicle to just about an acceptable limit of what was legal! By that, I mean no dashboard, no wiring, no brakes. They kindly left a steering wheel.

Obviously, I needed to take it to a mechanic who had never seen anything like it in his life.

'Where is this from?' He asked.

'A Met auction,' I replied.

'You do realise, don't you, that it has probably regularly gone over speed bumps at about 80 mph with twelve fat coppers in the back?'

I hadn't considered it.

'It's not good,' he said, stating what was now becoming the bleeding obvious.

Next, I took it to a carpenter to stick a double bed in it. Then, I added a sink. Some running water would be nice and a portable potty. It had only done 14,000 miles and was absolutely wrecked. I spent four grand on it. I know what you are thinking. Don't ever spend four grand on a second hand car!

The truth is that it *looked* quiet smart when it was finished. I figured I would keep it for a couple of years. That's what I thought.

My first outing was back up to Ayr. We will see how this goes up through the mountains of Cumbria on the M6. Give it a little run out.

It must have been around 2 a.m when I broke for a short stop at the Services. Why oh why did everything run smoothly every time until you made a pit stop? I am driving along and the gear stick just comes out in my hand.

But I am still going. Unbelievably, the vehicle shows no sign of abandoning me. What the fuck do I now? I am in the middle of nowhere in the middle of night. What would *you* do? I figure I have no choice but to keep on going until it gives up and if that coincides with the next service station, the all the better.

I have to call the AA. You can't drive a car with no gear stick. All it takes is someone to bump into me and I could be responsible for the deaths of many people. It hadn't stopped me pushing on of course until I found a safe place to stop and believe me, on that stretch of the M6 coming round those corners with those massive drops, there is no such thing as a safe place to stop.

'All the cogs are ruined,' the AA man put it bluntly.

Then he told me somebody had probably put it into reverse while going along at 40 mph which is just about the craziest thing I have ever heard and he had no way of knowing such garbage but obviously two things were true.

But, more importantly, the cogs and the gearstick were clearly so fucked it must have looked like that!

This was going to be one of those vehicles where every journey you would discover something new, no matter how many times your mechanic friend looked it over. Well, I still had to make it to Ayr! So, there was no other option but a bit of duct tape and a few screws shoving the thing back in and off I went gingerly leaving a bemused and disbelieving patrol man at the Services.

I limped into Scotland, knowing the brakes were failing. Smoke coming out of every part of the van needed no explanation. Never mind playing in a tournament, I have to get this thing safe and ready to attempt to get me home. I crawl into Kwik Fit where I am told it needs a special part and there is no way in the world I can drive it – a pretty unconvincing line to a man who has just come from Hastings but at least I am here now and have a few days of the tournament where there is no pressure to go anywhere.

I am knackered at this point having driven through the night with all the stress of it so I ask the Kwik Fit man if I can park up anywhere round here. He points me in the direction of a nice, quiet unadopted road round the back where I can get my head down. Brilliant, I will just settle down here for a bit and stay put until it is time to get down to the darts.

Wow – I could not have picked a less quiet 'unadopted' road. Not really in a position to go anywhere, I find I am a magnet for about 20 voices, and every bloody druggie and street-fighter in

Scotland. This is where they hung out at night oblivious to the fact that a man was trying to get some sleep before the next day's tournament.

As you might expect, when it came to the darts the next day, I was a shambles. Sometimes you can rise above everything that is going on in life and find solace in competition. At others you just couldn't leave it behind and the darts were no escape route with your whole mood in turmoil because of external pressures. This, apart from preparation and natural ability is probably the biggest stumbling block for sports people who play individual disciplines rather than team games. You have nobody to lift you and nowhere to go and I think many darts players struggled with this mental conundrum and money would have been a factor that would have been divisive. When you are spending so much cash just to get you to events, you therefore – alongside that burden – create a pressure on yourself to perform where you expectation often exceeds your ability.

I ended up blowing nearly 15K in a year on that van and none of it was worth it of course. You just keep feeding it so that you can get through to the next event or back home in one piece. Fifteen grand is about a sixth of my career earnings, for God's sake.

Case in point – the part they got me at Kwik Fit didn't work and I was forced to make my way home like a snail. All 469 miles. I didn't get any further than Clacket Lane Services on the

M25. It was an embarrassment. I had been getting overtaken by milk floats, it was that bad. I am now low on fuel and end up in the hard shoulder.

Irony, of all ironies…I see two flashing blue lights behind me. This should be fun, I am thinking. I would have put my own one on but the bastards ripped that out too.

'Get off the hard shoulder,' they shouted at me.

Easier said than done.

'Why are you driving this?' Thicko The Plod asked.

Clearly not for my own amusement.

'I am driving your van,' I laughed in their face without them really understanding why. Typical cop with attitude.

'If I see you on the motorway, I am going to arrest you,' he warned. 'You are to go no further.'

Well, I couldn't really risk it, could I? I would have done a few years before probably but I had no choice but to call a Hastings breakdown company who wanted another 600 notes to come and get me making this the single-most disastrous weekend in my darts history.

I decided to cut my losses by the time the van had run up about 25,000 miles and took it to my mate Richie, who managed a few players in the Birmingham area. God knows how it even got there but I told him I would get it to him then he was to get rid of it and I never wanted to see the heap of shit again.

It would generally run OK for about three months then all the bills would come at once. In the end I took about £1800 for it and decided that I was done with vans for good.

That lasted for about a year when I realised that I missed the life and set about getting another one but this time for different reasons...

Chapter Thirty-One

Quit

Phil Taylor had the class – no doubt about it. We were on the periphery of his greatness. By 2003, I was nearly tipped over the edge.

I had met him again in another final – notably the UK Open which was the real FA Cup of darts at The Reebok Stadium in Bolton which I loved because for once there was an open draw every round. None of this bullshit where the names come out of the hat and the die is cast all the way to the final. Pick them fresh every single tie – keeps it interesting for everybody. That's why most tournaments in the world, except tennis operate like this. They talk about the magic of the FA Cup – that is because Hastings could randomly get drawn against Manchester United.

I lie, of course, Manchester United are obviously not good enough to get out of the qualifying rounds into the main draw so a lucrative tie with my non-league hometown amateurs is something they can only go to bed at night and dream of!

Yet 2003 meant a watershed in my life and in my career. You could be runner-up in a final but still come away deflated. It didn't matter that you were therefore the second best player in that group in that week. You only knew that you hadn't won. That casts a grey spell on your mind and for all the good times, I knew that just over a decade from The Split, I was cracking up, the tank was empty and I had given it everything and despite improved conditions, terms and rewards, had still taken very little from the game.

I wanted out.

My darts had almost hit rock bottom too. And even when I was firing on all cylinders, which was less and less, I knew in my head that I was going through the motions. I was no longer in rhythm with the sport, the crowd or my competitors. I was robotic, not walking on with a swagger to the music but arriving at the oche with noise playing in the background. I was detached in every way.

It happens in many sports – all sports. Few go out at the top or chose the moment to do so. At some point, someone comes along who does new things and makes you look old and slow and daft, or you just fall out of synch with who you were whilst your expectations for life change around you.

All of this was happening in 2003.

Suddenly I had been forced to qualify again. I had to win £50 in the play offs to get in. In six or seven qualifying tournaments I hadn't won a penny. This was my last chance to get in the UK Open. We were back to Square One at an age when I really could

240

not be going in reverse.

I was resorting to playing in the pubs again. The former World Number Three was back where he had come from. I remember realising how far I had sunk when a load of Welsh boys turned up at a bar in Manchester and one of them worked for a pet food company. I was supposed to be a pro and here I am …not exactly a dog with a bone risking the last drops of my reputation against someone who sensed he could winalot.

There were eight of them. Then their driver walked in. He didn't ask me if I wanted a Port and Brandy. Times had changed. The Welsh boys paid for their driver to enter as a thank you for getting them there and back. Then the inevitable happened. I bloody drew him.

I am now resorting to having to beat the driver to qualify. I do, of course succeed but it was the only game I won. That was how low I had fallen in my skills and in my belief. I walked away with the £50 I needed. It wasn't quite Vegas or a televised final.

I hadn't got here overnight of course. It had been a gradual process really from 2001 onwards. I had blips when I thought I had reversed the trend, practising with Australian Tony and getting some sort of form back, thinking 'these are going in' but generally I was in decline. Phil was now a millionaire or well on his way to being one and I just kept thinking what on earth had gone wrong. I wasn't at his level – nobody was – but my ranking at one point was two behind him and yet now I was playing for

241

£50 and not even sure I could beat a minibus driver. It wasn't jealousy because he was a pro. I just couldn't figure out how it had only *nearly* happened for me.

My financial worth had come full circle – I hadn't got the big brewery contracts and I had never saved when the money was nearly really good. I was seriously facing the prospect of never throwing a dart again.

I boarded a plane to Chicago, thinking I just do not want to do this any more. When we landed, I sat in the hotel room and I felt a cold coming on. Stupid really – because a cold wouldn't stop you playing yet realistically five Ports and Brandys probably should have several times. I never shot a single dart. I didn't want to play. I just made out I was too poorly to turn out.

Maybe I was – in the head. I was depressed. Life hadn't beaten me. Darts had. I had never considered there might be at some point one without the other. A life with darts – apart from the pool years – just seemed inevitable until the day I died.

I could feel myself fading away. I couldn't get myself up for it. I slid way down the rankings outside of the elusive 32. That meant that the TV tournaments were gone. The pressure in my head was relentless…the voices too were playing havoc. One minute all I was hearing was 'shit, I'm in decline'…the next 'you can get this back'. I didn't know what to think except that it is a terrible sinking feeling when you are fighting your mind and can no longer visualise that swagger that was for so long part of you.

You tell yourself you are just one good match away from getting it all back but that game never comes.

So by the skin of my enormous arse, I managed to qualify for the UK Open and told Roland Sholten things were going well but also that heads were going to roll and that I was going to take somebody out. I was talking the talk. At the same time, I wasn't even convincing myself and just began to believe I was shit – yet I was telling Roland I was serious and something was going to happen.

Darts was a pretty cocksure business where you drunk booze, drove home on it and in a working man's environment, banter never beat you – you gave it back. Now, I was questioning everything but acting aggressively, punching my way out of my mind. That is nothing to do with the way the sport is played or the characters attracted to it – it just a classic fall from grace story that befalls every sportsman at some point and it is a mental health issue about acceptance of who you were and who you were becoming.

It is not ego – it is disappointment and failure to adjust. So, this testosterone level which was really starting to peak wasn't a hostile new angry me but more a desperate cry for help, clinging on just about to whatever was slipping away. To a degree, I could see my Dad and the way he all but excelled and then abandoned darts to golf and back again.

Does luck play a part in an attempt to make a comeback?

Maybe, you do a need little break to believe again but essentially you either still have the arrows or you don't. I was 5-0 down against Andy Belton and won 6-5. That score line tells you everything – that I still had it to bulldoze an opponent but then when it came to it, I struggled to get over the line. Sport is mental. And when I did, victory was almost hollow because my mind had subsided to the point where I had nearly chucked it away – and that is where fatigue comes in. You think about those Ports and Brandys and the way you glide into a final without a care in the world and then when you throw away a lead the weight of the burden exhausts you. It was not fun hanging on.

But, things were getting a little better. Just, a little.

I drew Cliff Lazaranko in the last 16. Here is a man on form today. He is beating me convincingly. There is no way back if I am honest.

Then luck does intervene.

The fire alarm goes off. What were the chances of that? Well, I am surprised it hadn't happened more often with the pissed up people at darts. We're all outside in the heatwave for about half an hour and guess what, it's a false alarm!

We re-enter the venue and Cliff is just not the same player. I beat him hands down. Do darts turn on moments like this? I am in the semi and it's an open draw.

Eric is in charge of the live draw on the stage! It is down to Phil, Roland, a local lad from Bolton named Paul Williams and myself. I am pretty sure I know who I want to play. This is rank amateur stuff now as Eric puts four bits of paper in a trophy. It was like being back in the pub in Hastings – nothing sophisticated or professional about this. You could almost see the names under the corners of the paper. I mean this is ridiculous. A Semi-Final with Phil Taylor in it and we are working on a nod and a wink. The crowd and Sky, of course, wanted a Phil versus the local lad final – the fairy tale stuff. They were egging Eric on. Well I never. The draw came out. Phil versus Roland and myself versus Paul Williams. Then, naturally the natives got restless as their boy got dumped out. Their tournament was over. For me, it was just beginning.

I was in the final against the powerhouse and even though I had pulled on all my mental strength and a fading ability, something was nagging me that this was my last crack at Phil Taylor. All that mockery with the Ports and Brandys and all my own struggles indicated that it was now or never. Yet, something sparkled that day.

The mental disintegration that Phil had cast over me when I had been close to the top of my game was in stark contrast to that nothing to lose mentality when I had disintegrated of my own accord. I stopped being meek and fragile and definitely played better than in any other final against Phil.

Phil took an early lead. I mounted a fightback. We were neck and neck for six legs. I even smashed in a 170 finish. I really believed this was it now. The turning point. I was marching back. Suddenly I felt happy again. Not for long… and even though Phil did beat me, I got £15,000 for losing in the final. I thought this would lead to better things.

But when the dust settled, I felt otherwise. I used the money to do some urgent repairs on my house and that in itself depressed me. I was *back* but I just knew deep down that I couldn't do it any more. I didn't have the time or funds to commit to getting *back* back. I don't know if it was the end of the road or I had talked myself down a one way street, but I do know this – just like my Dad, once you've told yourself that there is no way back, the battle is all in the mind and that is a road twice as hard to climb as a loss of form.

I *had* lost some skill but it was not as though I had arthritis. Not yet anyway. I was probably still there more or less but the edge had gone from my character and my persona. I didn't feel part of that crowd any more in terms of ability nor in terms of road trips, bar trips and Vegas trips.

Something had just given.

I sold my latest campervan, borrowed some money off my Mum and took a test to get an HGV license. Then I got a job driving. I knew that I could now always work – unless I fucked up my license.

I dropped out of my local team and all competitive action and only played here and there. I turned to agency work, including driving off road for a company called Reprotec which meant as the dust carts would come in and the rubbish would be dumped on the floor, Reprotec would take it up to Hastings Tip.

Then, a bizarre thing happened. I got word from my local landlord, Dick Morten, that the Community Centre at Pebsham had won the contract to host Sussex County Darts.

'I know you don't do county darts any more…but I need someone to do the catering,' he tailed off.

I had never cooked in my life. Other than for myself. Not 150 people anyway!

So, I offered.

'I'll have a crack at it,' I beamed ignorantly.

What did this really mean? I don't know if I can cook for so many. I can't even fucking play darts any more and now I am going into a darts venue cooking. It was madness.

I spoke with my mate Cardy's wife, Sharon, who worked as a dinner lady at a local school. She agreed to come in with me and 'acquire some chips, pasta, rice, margarine etc' and we would do it together!

Then I revealed the plan behind my cunning signature dish.

'I can find most of the meat we need over at the tip.'

No response.

It was one of those statements which was left hanging in the air in a sort of 'I'll not ask any questions' kind of way.

I knew the truth was as grim as it sounds. Once a week the

guys in the Asda lorry would give me the heads-up they were on the way and pull up and dump the lot, and off it would toddle to its next destination. I would pull up in my truck and raid the lot – at just a couple of days out of date, there were chicken legs, bacon and salad a plenty. Yes, salad, really. Only the seagulls were fighting me for it.

The daft thing was the council employed a guy to scare them away. That was his job and he was on the payroll.

In the summer months he would just stand there in his pants and a pair of Wellingtons cracking a whip with items he had made from the tip. That job was great for me as it was all about the Asda truck rocking up!

In the winter, he would wear three or four items of clothing he had found in the rubbish and stick a pair of women's tights on his head. Well – he always seemed happy. It was the perfect deal. And now I was about to feed county players on supermarket rejects I had sifted through other rubbish for!

I thought my lodger and I had better test it out first! If we got poorly, then maybe not. If we survived then this was the way forward. I was now official caterer to the next generation of stars!

We never got ill once.

Game on. Not literally. Asda didn't do game.

But for a poultry sum…boom boom…in other words, the cost of a baguette in the morning, Burgess Catering was up and running.

I got everything off the tip and, in a way, it restored my happiness that darts had robbed me off. I am not sure why but I think it was the concept of getting away with the tip run, the fact that it tasted good, the bonus that it cost nothing and the payoff that I was being paid for feeding players who were doing exactly what I had started out doing.

I started to up my game. This time I do mean game. My mate shot deer. He distributed it cheaply. It wasn't dear. Too many bloody puns here. Sharon and I did a roast venison with all the trimmings.

No takers – it was too rich, or they didn't like venison they claimed.

The truth is the heathens had never tried it at all.

I was not to be beaten. When I got home, I chopped the lot up and made it into a stew. I would try again the next day. I was not about to get in a stew about getting it in a stew – wherever it came from.

I re-appeared the following morning and announced my cunningly disguised, freshly prepared re-hash of yesterday's tea.

Lamb stew became my forte!

Guess what, they ate the whole fucking thing.

As long as those boys from DEFRA didn't come knocking on anyone's door, nobody was any the wiser. It always went down a storm and everybody hoofed the lot. For that avoidance of doubt, that doesn't mean I was cooking horsemeat either even though it is well documented that some of supermarkets have used that in the past couple of decades.

Did any of the players even know? Pigs might fly. If they did of course, they would end up in the pot too. All they wanted were their darts, their beers and their food. A hot pot was a hot pot and nobody asked any questions! Even though it was a re-branding of the night before!

I look back now and laugh and some of these players will be reading this for the first time blissfully unaware that I literally pulled a rabbit out of a hat. At the time, it helped me a lot. I took my eyes off the arrows and marvelled at the pots. I was into catering and not playing. The former took the pain from the latter.

Sadly, whilst my eyes had been opened to the possibilities ahead, it didn't last forever – principally because Dick passed away. He loved his darts and just wanted to put on a good show. With his demise, the club soon followed and that, in essence, represented part of the old school amateurism of the sport. If centred around one person just and they went, so did the glue.

Darts, in more ways than one, was full of dicks. Limpdick at school gave me the platform. Eric's manager Dick put me on it. And now poor old Dick's death pulled the rug on my little scheme and release from the game.

Losing Dick was a blow in so many ways – a fantastic guy who really put his neck on the line for me. If anyone had ever found out exactly what we had been up to with the catering then it would have opened a massive can of worms that would have had Dick closed down.

Unless, of course, the worms looked edible and I could somehow work them into my next recipe.

Chapter Thirty-Two

Alternating

I have to find another life. Darts – just like the cops did when they ripped out my nightmare of a van – had taken a back seat. I had finally fallen out of the ratings and even though my mates had been warning me not to slip outside of the promised land of the Top 32, I didn't really take it on board and always thought that if I just pulled myself together, I could waltz back in there.

But, I was in decline and before you know it you are no longer even in the Top 50. For the first time, I wanted a motorhome for the right reasons. I liked the lifestyle and I didn't want to always remember those miles on the roads as being about struggles to get from A to B and the disappointment of coming home empty-handed. I wanted to take all that pressure off me and see what it felt like to use the thing for the reasons it was intended for.

I did what any sensible man would do in the middle of a mid-life crisis. I took eighteen grand out of the house, converted them into Euros, rang my cousin Mick and booked a trip to buy my latest motorhome…in Hamburg. Let's go marry a virgin and have some steak! The bizarre thing about this trip was that the trip back was the safest I had ever driven. I have been deaf in my left ear since I was five. Sorry? I said I have been deaf in my left ear since I was five. Don't worry, I have heard it all before – or not as the case may be.

But, driving the left hand drive from Germany meant that for the first time in my life, I did not have to turn my right ear across to hear whatever garbage my passenger was dribbling on about at the time, which normally meant because I was twisted all the way round I would end up swerving across the road. What were the chances of that? A van that drove safely and a driver who did the same. For about the first time in my life.

I had picked up this fantastic little left-hand drive European vehicle. They all look amazing when you pick them up, don't they? But this van more than any represents the line in the sand between nomadic darts player and tourist. I had a couple of great trips and a couple of disasters – standard fare really – but as ever the two banes in my life scuppered my plans. Darts and women!

I would soon meet my wife Michelle, who was required to be kept in the standard of living she was accustomed to and that didn't mean slinging the things in the back of a van at a moment's notice. She liked the trips but it was time to impose some order on my life.

And, despite my decline in form, I still had enough in me to qualify for The World Masters. I didn't have the belief which is why I had booked to go on a little tour round Cornwall, Somerset and Devon which was to be *our* big campervan trip together. No darts, no hares!

When you are slipping away from the big elite bunch of players, you still just have enough in you in that first year in decline to pull yourself back and even though I was playing with zero expectation possibly to the point where I was that relaxed because I almost didn't care, I won the Sheppey Classic and that meant part of the reward was that I qualified for The World Masters in Rotherham! At that stage, I actually would have been happy with a Chicken Dinner as my prize. Irony of all ironies. I really didn't fancy putting myself out there and did fancy the road trip to the South West.

Fucking Rotherham when I could have been in Cornwall. The two weeks clashed. Yet again, darts won the day. No trip to the West Country. Wife mightily pissed off. With that, her heart was never in the van again. So, I make my way up to Rotherham with my mate Wonky Eye Jason in a little Citroen I then had. With his eye and my ear, together we just about had a full set! Guess what…

The alternator goes in the car. I think now this is one of the reasons I fell out of love with darts. It was bad enough not being able to crack Phil's dominance but I couldn't get to the bloody tournaments in one piece most of the time.

I spend £250 on a new alternator. When I get there, I play

brilliantly all day. I lose my first game on the stage in the Last Sixteen to Jamie 'Yosser' Hughes. I get £250. That about sums it up. I knew there and then that is why I never got anywhere in this game.

There was nothing I could do about it now and yes sometimes I did have regrets and thought maybe I was a bit unlucky. Phil and Eric had supreme talent but also lived in the right part of the country. The Midlands or the North East were the places were darts were thriving and I am all the way down in Hastings. You can't help where you grow up but it hindered how I grew as a darts player. They also seemed to be able to tap into those big brewery contracts which were just elusive to most of us. It propelled Eric into such super stardom that he even appeared on the first ever National Lottery programme. He paved the way for super stardom and the breakaway and Phil became the next legend of darts.

You play alongside these characters and room and drink with them but it is only really at the end of your career when you see the gulf and have the odd regret. They were brilliant players who have made the most of their talent and image. I didn't have enough mental nous to compete with them for sustained periods of time. But I did know one thing. Devon was nicer than Rotherham and I was better than driving in a clapped-out vehicle, getting humiliated, and seeing my fee disappear straight back into funding my transport.

Chapter Thirty-Three

A Soft Tip Off From The Powers That Be

Bravedart had been in touch – a dart's player's mobile just read like a comic book of names but this was of course was Jamie Harvey.

'There's a soft tip tournament in Chicago in a couple of weeks' time,' he mooted, gauging interest.

It really was like this. No agents or a governing body dictating your diary. You knew when the inked-in big ones were but if you got wind of a potential trip and the chance of a bit of cash with an added dose of fun, you just got on a plane and went – as long as you weren't going to be too down on the deal.

I told him that apart from gate-crashing a couple of Mickey Mouse tournaments in the States, I had never played soft tip in my life.

So, obviously I said yes.

I rang a friend of mine in New York called Neil Dixon – Neil was hairdresser to the stars but also a very keen darts player. Whenever a trip like this came up we all started calling in favours of second-guessing where there might be a bed for the night and the cheapest way to get there so I told Neil I was coming in via Toronto and asked him to pick me up…despite the fact that I was heading for Chicago. Why not stop in the Big Apple on the way!

It is a stifling 90 degrees in the shade in Toronto. The news tells me that there is really bad weather in New York so I look at the map but it only looks an inch away. I decided to board and there are only six of us on the plane. From take-off, the clouds get blacker and blacker. It is up and down and sideways all the way – one of those rides when you think that if you are going to get out of here alive, you will play your best darts ever and make peace with all your enemies, just thankful to be alive.

That elation at landing and all that good intent of how you would save the world if you made it of course soon turns to rat shit when you come through the dump that is LaGuardia to find…no Neil.

I am two hours late but everyone waiting on a plane can see that information. I try to call him. No answer. This is all you fucking need. 11:30 at night. New York. No pick-up. Oh, and they lost my bag too.

How can a plane with just six people on it forget your stuff? That leaves me with just my passport and $20. As I am sure you are aware, you won't even get a hello out of a New York cabbie for that price – and then he will want tipping.

Next thing – the airport is closing. One security guy offers to help me out if I can tell him where I am staying but I can only reply that I do not know where I am going unless this guy picks me up.

They have no choice therefore but to throw me out. Into the rain. With no coat. I survived the flight with good intention but now I realise that is just a warning. This is the night that I am going to die.

I am sat there, outside the airport gates, trying to gather myself but one over-riding thought persists. You are fucked, mate. All that goes through my head is will I get mugged, beaten or shot – or all three?

Yes, I was tired and yes, I was abandoned, stranded broke, wet, cold in a city of so many people where nobody could help me but I know that it was bigger than that. This moment was the crystal ball. This was the sign. All those years and all those miles for a collection of pennies and tin-pot trophies, chicken dinners and electric bench grinders. Striving to have a good time, provide a good life and keep your head above water had crashed headlong into a decline in form and appetite and the knowledge that it was slipping away. I ended up here for a bit of travel, some easy money and pressure-free darts. But where in fact was I? This was the road to nowhere. It was a dead-end street. It was the end of the line.

It didn't really matter that it was this particular moment in time or that the near-death plane experience had given me a little warning and now this was the final straw, it was of course all the build up to this that had been simmering for a couple of years that you try to deny – all that stuff about slipping out of the Top 32 and the 'I'll get back' mentality, a few gentle slips down the ladder and you are right at its foot.

In every sense – from my geographical and financial isolation stranded in New York to my own mental state, this was rock bottom. Life that had been racing by in the good times but now it crawled. A little sob followed by a pull yourself together, a pace up and down then a sit back where you where, thinking Neil is going to drive round that corner at any moment or he is never coming at all. Every minute lasted an eternity. You tell yourself, it will get light soon and with that will come some renewed hope and the likelihood of help but there was no basis for that really. If anything, in broad daylight you would just mingle in with all the other people on the street looking for help. I really did not know what to do in the short term and the whole question of the future looked even bleaker now. I couldn't keep trotting off round the world for a few dollars here and there...if indeed I could even make it out of here to get wherever *there* was.

I had stopped pricking up at the sound of a car coming round the corner by the time Neil pulled up three hours later. He was three hours *late* – *after* my delayed flight. He had seen on the equivalent of Teletext that our plane was coming in way beyond schedule, then got caught in traffic and now turned up in the dead of the night.

I had never been so pleased to see somebody whom I hardly knew at all.

'Thank fuck for that,' I greeted him. 'I really didn't think you were coming.'

It momentarily parked the general doom and gloom. In fact, of course, the tricks of the mind do more than temporarily shelve your problems. Relief like this is exactly the same as the 'if I ever get off this plane alive' syndrome. The future plans and gratitude you display in despair soon evaporate. That means you do not address the bigger picture. Sat there in the pissing down rain was another wake-up call to tell me this was all over. Being picked up made me think how bloody lucky I was and that the stars were shining on me. I would, of course, keep going now believing these were all signs talking myself into territory that I had been given one last chance. It was all bollocks of course. A storm across North America and my mate being delayed in traffic plus an airline losing my bag had fuck all to do with the fact that I was no longer a bulldog and most of the time my darts had become a load of shitzu.

So, when Neil left me at Hotel 17 in the district of Chelsea at a place with no TV, no lights and no hot water, I really felt a million dollars. None of it mattered. I did raise it with the concierge – even that was too grand a title for the man on reception – but was told if I wanted added extras like light, TV and hot water, they came at a further $10 each. I went to bed in the dark in silence in my clothes. Four days later, my bag turned up.

This kind of story was not uncommon amongst myself or my fellow pros. Cutting corners and doing it on the cheap often caught up with you. It was any wonder at all that you could actually throw a dart after all the bloody troubles getting there. This was no sightseeing trip to New York. I should have been in Chicago with Jamie and the two Peters.

By the time, I rocked up with them it turned out that the windy city was hosting a tournament that was full of hot air. Soft tip darts meant a maximum of 18 grams. I usually played with 22s. It was alien to everything I knew but we were pretty sure we had the nous and experience to win – and that meant $5000 in the bag. If of course, you were even allowed to play.

You could either enter the amateur or pro event. For the purposes of this tournament, we were the former.

We are told to wait at the back with all the amateur players before being called up one at a time. None of us minded of course but you didn't get this at the World Matchplay! It was the way they did things round here but also was a chance for them to weigh up the competition – which of course dawned on us as we approached the table at the front:

'We know who you are,' the man with the clipboard eyeballed Jamie. 'You're a pro.'

Then he said the same to Peter Evison and looked at me out

of the corner of my eye equally dismissively.

'You're Shayne Burgess. You're a pro too. No, you're not playing. You've got to play in the Pro event.'

At least I was still held in some regard.

Then – here's the best bit. He looked at Peter Manley who had a higher ranking than all of us and was a former World Number 2, and he never said a word. Peter walked straight in to the Amateur event and duly won it.

This was not the first time this had happened of course. They always ended up letting you in and it was often kudos for them to tell the story of how the pro Brits had come over and lost. Any one of them would fancy your scalp. The fact that you even entered gave the other players a boost. We were automatically insulting the amateurs just by turning up and thinking these were easy pickings! They were up for taking you out.

Nobody remembers most of the results at tournaments like this, despite the bragging rights and the standoffishness when you try to enter. It was a real eye opener and the local red necks were out in force. Continual whooping, and high-fiving. The further down the road you got, the more Ireland it became. That meant there was always a Tasmanian Devil round the corner.

This was what we call a double elimination tournament so if you lost twice, you were out and Dayton Strawbridge was the Tasmanian Devil who sent me packing. The name alone probably inspires an image. If I added that he spent the whole time chewing on his tobacco from underneath his baseball cap and that locals knew him as Satan Drawbridge, then that probably completes the picture.

'Now you can fuck off home,' replaced the customary handshake at the moment of his victory.

He spat whatever he was chewing out in my direction.

'Don't worry,' I replied. 'You've got to lose twice yet and you will lose so I will see you in the next round.'

That's exactly what happened. Second time around, he lost and I drew him again. I destroyed him. Probably, not the best plan in the world.

Beer, which the locals had paid good money for – a waste I had seen a thousand times before – starts to fly everywhere. The spectators are rolling around in it, partying in the fountains and rubbishing a very decent hotel. I suspect they had done this a thousand times before too.

I lost my second elimination game a couple of rounds later. Takings $100. Get your prize money and the hell out of there!

There was a lot more soft tip darts in America than at home. I didn't really like the rules and it wasn't what I was brought up on. In fact, often I couldn't take it seriously. I was playing in the mixed pairs with Jessica Nicholl, the granddaughter of one of the steel tip organisers Bill and I think this must have been the point when I decided that it was all a bit daft and apart from the money, there was nothing real about it, so I went out and bought myself a

Tommy Cooper style fez hat to play in.

I didn't really think much of it, other than it added to the pantomime of the tournament. I certainly wouldn't have turned up in Blackpool to play dressed like that even though, of course it was perfect for that kind of crowd. I think it shows, though harmless, I didn't really rate it.

For the record, Jessica and I lost in the Mixed Pairs Final and Jamie and I lost in the Mens Pairs. A double dose of defeat.

And that meant it was time to go home. The clues were all there again. Horrendous electrical storms meant that I was stuck on the runway for two hours waiting for the storm to blow over. The pilot kept telling us they would update the passengers every twenty minutes. Everyone just looked at each other to say we won't be taking off in this. Then, of course, it got worse. The Captain made a decision to leave in a hurry and we were up and down with turbulence all the way home, seat belts never off.

When we landed finally, I too made a decision.

I can't do this anymore. I am not going back to America. I can't do this or the U.S.A again. I turned on the news and a plane had come down in that storm in Dallas, Texas. As it does to most people when they see that, it puts you off long haul flying for a while but the truth of the matter is that this had been a trip of scrapes and plenty of signs to read in to that after several false starts at both giving up and then a brief re-birth of form, it really was time to quit.

I thought about my Dad, who despite not being a pro, somehow found the ability to pack up altogether and walk away. It had been my life. I wasn't sure if I would ever *or* never throw a dart again. I just knew the *game* was up.

When I got home, there was another letter waiting for me. It was from the PDC, forwarded on from the American equivalent. The organisers had reported me for wearing a fez. Even though it was fine for the rednecks to wear their hats.

My behaviour on my recent trip was not becoming of a professional in the finals. Unbelievable.

They had done really well to dob me in from the middle of Chicago to *my* governing body about a tournament nobody back home really cared. You had to take your hat off to them. Of course, if I had taken my hat off we wouldn't have this problem.

Chapter Thirty-Four

Fade To Gray

I concluded that there were only so many times you could be kicked in the teeth. I knew that I had been going through the motions. I had free-fallen out of the rankings. I didn't love it one bit any more. It was all I knew and by 2004, it really was all over.

It just took a bit of time to realise. Probably because I had something more tangible to hang that hat on, I couldn't just give up overnight like Dad did. But then again, maybe that it is how it appeared on the surface. Perhaps when he finished, it had been brewing inside him for some time.

For me, all the travelling and the strain on relationships and not really having much to show for it meant that by the time I finally spoke those words 'I am going to call it a day' I did so with immense relief.

I was starting to get the first signs of arthritis and RSI meant that at times I felt like my arm was falling off. My eyes and back were going too and this meant that the mental concentration was shot to pieces. I was crabby at home and had lost interest in most things – especially darts.

I decided to go to the opticians and explained what I did but that now I could no longer hit a pig's arse with a shovel. I had in effect lost all hand to eye co-ordination. I asked him – almost pleaded with him to help. I undertook a full-on half an hour eye test.

Finally, the optician piped up:

'I've got good news and bad news,' he begun ominously. 'The good news is that you have 20:20 vision.'

'OK, what's the bad news?' I replied.

'You're just a shit darts player.'

In fact, one realisation that hits you is that you are now faced with a gigantic void. My hobby became my living. It wasn't to be any more. I therefore no longer had a hobby nor a living. To even make the Top 200 in darts and other sports like golf etc, you had to have that selfish focus which meant that it was the game at all costs and everything fell by the wayside and even those people who were nowhere good enough to penetrate the Top 32 at some point held that dream, that vision and ambition and that relentless pursuit of it.

As I said earlier, you don't consider the downside of the mountain when you are storming up it in the good times.

I think most people know when it is time to quit and when they realise, they look back and understand they have been hanging on and that moment was actually defined for them some time before.

I would have probably cut off all together if it hadn't been a chance meeting with my old mate Mark Card and his daughter Abby. She had started seeing a guy called Adrian Gray. They say life comes in circles – well, here was the proof. The Card family had always been darts crazy and now had bought Adrian into the fold as they had reeled me in when I was at school.

I saw something in him which I liked. I had been a late starter at the game but Adrian was in his early 20s and wanted to better himself, which around Sussex on the circuit was rare and exactly the reason I had moved to the Kent leagues. So, almost reluctantly, I got sucked in and began to play pairs with him when really I couldn't be bothered to at all. I was pissed off with the game but pissed off that I was pissed off.

I guess I was sulking. I know I became very highly strung.

Strangely, playing with Adrian turned something around even though I was never going back. I had sold my last campervan and was now working in the sewers. Adrian was, and is, a carpet fitter but in no time at all had gone from Sussex League to inside the Top 32 beating Phil Taylor live on TV – something I had never managed to achieve. That made everyone stand up. Some years later, he became the World's Number One soft tip player. Just to rub it in, he lives opposite me now! Along with Rob Cross. Don't get me wrong – Rob and Adrian aren't shacked up together. It just now seemed that Hastings was Dartsville Central.

By the way – Adrian is The Conqueror and Rob is The Voltage.

Whatever.

But I was ecstatic for him even though our lives were passing each other on an escalator. He was going up and racing towards the top. I was plummeting downwards and getting off at the bottom. I *was* genuinely pleased for him and in effect he nursed me out of my career. I can understand why people just stop. It takes everything out of you. You hear of many sportsmen who never pick up a bat or a club again. But, when it has been your life you probably should try to find a way to stay involved and realistically, he kept me sharp enough to not just disappear like a sad sack of shit and I really wanted to drive him on to heights that I hadn't reached.

It did help me.

It takes a fair bit in life and sport to will somebody else on, even when you have had the camaraderie of room-sharing as we did for so much of the tour but when you get to a mindset that you realise the next best thing to you succeeding is to help or encourage someone you feel close to, to go on to better what you did then that is also an amazing sensation. Just like any Dad with any son. Just like my Dad with me.

It is also far too fucking mature for Burgess.

Our relationship was genuine and Adrian was that person and I was delighted to be best man at his wedding and will happily be so for any future weddings he may have. This is darts, after all.

Inevitably, I made sure that the main course on the day was a chicken dinner.

One thing that I didn't realise at the time and I think only the very calculating sportsmen do is that there *is* another life and darts can be part of that and once you step out of tournament play, you can become poacher turned gamekeeper and your notoriety and status can in fact increase. There *is* another life.

So, I get a call saying that Wayne 'Hawaii 501' Mardle has dropped out and can I get to London to do the Ruby Wax TV show. They need a darts player. Presumably anybody fitting the stereotype who can just about aim an arrow in the right direction. Without a fucking surf board. Do I want to do it?

I drive myself to London. It is freezing cold. I am hanging around waiting. The next thing…I am in the green room with Matthew Kelly, Harry Enfield and a load of women from the TV show of the day *Footballers Wives*. I don't think any of them know who I am and I am pretty sure Ruby is clueless too. I am a nobody to them. I am clearly just a prop. In fact, they don't have any props at all. They told me to bring a board along.

Ruby invites me into her changing room cum boudoir and asks me if I know what I was there for. I said no!

'Every week I have someone on with a different talent…last week this guy plucked a pheasant. The week before we had a working loom. This week, it's a darts player. You are going to teach me how to throw darts.'

I would have probably been more suited to fucking plucking a pheasant.

They had painted the studio luminous green in what they think resembles a darts environment. It was a piss take really.

So, I am not allowed to throw any warm up darts and begin to play beat the score with three darts. She has never thrown a dart in her life and it showed. Ignoring everything I told her, she throws right-handed with her left foot forward shouting at me to not tell her what to do.

Roll cameras.

I go first and hit one, Treble one and Single 20. Grand total – 24. Fuck. Total humiliation imminent.

Ah yes, this is Ruby Wax we are talking about. She lines up with cack-handed stance. Dart one flies over the board and takes out the cameraman at the back. Dart two goes into the floor. Stone cold sober for once, I am laughing my head off thinking I am safe here when she throws Double Twelve. Bollocks it's a tie. This apparently masquerades as entertainment. I feel numb at the experience. But it opens my mind to possibilities and I realise that I am just about moving on. Ruby Wax no. Ruby Port, maybe.

Louis Theroux' researchers rung too with a view to spending one of those *Weird Weekends* with me.

'I hear you eat squirrels,' she began. 'Can Louis come and stay?'

'That's right,' I replied. 'I shoot them in the crematorium at dusk.'

She never called back.

Of course, one thing a lot of sports people talk about when they finish is this notion of giving something back. I didn't feel I owed darts anything. Plus – I had already regurgitated most of those fucking chicken dinners the night I ate them. But, I did have a couple of meetings with the PDC over the years and knew that I had a lot to offer from the purely practical experience of having been a jobbing darts man.

It was all very well being an administrator but had you ever driven home at 2 am from the end of the earth with no money in your pocket and the fuel light flashing on a motor that is not roadworthy having been dumped out of a tournament in the first round? Almost definitely not.

There were also a lot of players' meetings over the years that the public would never be aware of but if you think about The Split – albeit led by a few colourful and dominant characters – and factor in that we almost always travelled together, there was a body and a voice amongst the elite players even though we were all competing with each other. Few of us had that business nous to eloquently represent ourselves but we did meet regularly.

One of the more bizarre points of contention as these meetings often descended from the very well-meaning practical to a raucous free for all at the end was Phil's presence on stage.

There were a lot of rumblings about him.

You would probably be fair to guess that much of this came from jealousy the better he got. Yet he was so intense that during a match he was practically breathing down your neck. He would stand so close to you that he was permanently in your shadow and almost click your heel as you walked to the board to retrieve your darts. I don't think he even realised he did it.

We were supposed to be discussing TV contracts and better pay but here we were asking if we should have a second oche behind the oche.

'You can't leave the second one until the first one has been vacated,' I proposed.

'Shut up Burgess, you are fucking idiot, you can't have two oches.' I was firmly told.

A couple of years after…what happened?

There were two different colours of carpets and an exclusion zone!

Sometimes you do only effect change by being the bastard who speaks up.

By 2017, some stupid voice in my head convinced me to have another crack at the circuit. That notion of a comeback was something anyone retired had a long time to think about. You might see someone on the box and think 'well surely I am still better than him' or you might have a really good Friday night where you – and others without the knowledge – tell you that 'it looks like the old magic is back' and before you know it, the scenario is churning around in your head that actually it is far from out of the question. You allow yourself to dream those dreams which propelled you there in the first place, except this time you are coming at them from a different angle.

When you start, you don't know how far you can go and you lie awake thinking about the possibilities. By the time you have finished and you only have flashback, you cling to former glories of individuals darts you threw from the hundreds of thousands of darts you have flung and they replay constantly in your head without any understanding of two key points.

You arm is not what it used to be. More importantly, your mind is far from sharp any more. You are literally out of the game. Once you make that decision to come back though, nobody is going to stop you. It is an individual sport full of crazy people. You make so many of the decisions on your own. Nobody was going to stop me having one last shot at the big time.

Except the opposition.

That was the one element I hadn't really considered. Yes – I had seen enough to think I had a sniff again. But I hadn't really understood that it was a totally different world now. In five to six years, the standard had gone through the roof in every aspect from preparation to performance. A lot more players were putting in a lot more practise.

I would give it another shot. I would be Status Quo with

another comeback tour. I had four chances to qualify outright for the Tour Card.

On the first day of Q School (qualifying school), I made my way to Robin Hood Park in Wigan and then lost 6-1. It couldn't get any worse and the months of bigging yourself up to this moment made me feel like I was taking the piss out of myself. I went back to the hotel and this time did not pace around the room or break down sobbing.

I had a serious word with myself about my attitude.

'You're better than this,' I reminded myself.

But was I recalling a time in the past or assessing where I was today?

Over the next few days, I did play exceptionally well, claiming some very decent scalps. That would have put me inside the – get this – Top 128 but it would have been enough to open doors. Nearly, but not quite. In the end I fell about four to five points short of getting back on the circuit.

With a few more hours and a more contemporary approach that I could learn from watching some of the new kids off the block, I could tweak this. I really could break back inside that circle and start all over again.

I started to dream once more…

Chapter Thirty-Five

Not A Bullseye Finish

And that was about two years ago! I still wake up most mornings and wonder, and I now do play regularly. In the period that passed, I thought about going back to the BDO though they play most of their tournaments abroad in places like Denmark, Austria and Finland which I really didn't fancy any more.

Once you step off the treadmill, it takes a lot to get back on it. I didn't want to be on a plane every other weekend. It really was a younger man's game. But generally, I didn't have the time or the headspace to commit to giving it another go. You really do need a lot of energy to come back from the dead.

Plus, I had to earn a living. That always stood at the heart of everything I ever worked for and given that darts had been my life and I wasn't really trained for much else, or indeed *anything* else. I was now driving a shit tanker and often that was through the night. To be clear, when I say *shit tanker* this is not the latest in crappy vehicles I had purchased. My living was now clearing blockages of fat in the sewers and moving it to another sewer! My career had gone from bull to shit.

Bullshit.

Before you know it, so much time has passed and you are so far out of the game you feel like a spectator again back in Mum and Dad's flat watching Jocky Wilson where it all started and with barely any memory of leaving JW flat out in a bar in Chicago. Much like the man himself that afternoon.

I was playing really good darts but I knew that I wasn't getting any younger and that I couldn't do it consistently.

You get to the point where you are not prepared to make the sacrifices needed nor do you back yourself to get up again after taking a hammering.

But you still dare to dream. As I write this, I have probably made the biggest life–changing decision of them all. Despite a life on the road, I always went back to Hastings. In 2019, my second wife Michelle (who is not an avid darts fan though predictably I did meet her at a darts tournament) and I have decided to move to St. Helens.

It couldn't really get more left-field than that after all these years but of course, there was one key element in me agreeing to the move. I was as close as I could be to Robin Park in Wigan where the PDC play about 80% of their tournaments. I haven't told the missus this of course. She thinks we are moving closer to her family. I have one eye on the latest comeback!

The dream never dies. The flame still burns a little. The trousers don't fit. The campervans are no more. Rabbits and hares still fear me!

Plus...everyone still gets fifteen quid. In fact, they get a whole lot more. This bulldog might just be biting back one more time soon...

The End

The Final Course

Life on the road meant I was always stocked with non-perishables, my gun, and fishing rod. Always ready to cook. Below are a few of my go-to recipes:

Rabbit And Lager Curry

Ingredients:

1 Whole rabbit, skinned and jointed

4 large onions

1 teaspoon of minced garlic

1 teaspoon of minced ginger

1 teaspoon of ground coriander

1 teaspoon of ground cinnamon

1 teaspoon of turmeric

4 Cardamom pods

1 teaspoon of paprika

1 teaspoon of Garam masala

1 teaspoon of medium curry powder

1 teaspoon of salt

Dry chillies

1 400ml Can of lager

1 teaspoon of palm sugar

1 tablespoon of corn flour

1 tub of Elmlea Double cream

Method:

Finely slice 4 onions

Sweat them down in oil for 15 minutes

Don't brown onions – just translucent

Add 3 chopped tomatoes

Stir 10-15 minutes

Stir in garlic & ginger

Stir 5 mins

Put in coriander and cumin and turmeric

Cardamom pods

Paprika

Garam masala

Curry powder

Put a tablespoon spoon of cornflour in

Put salt in

Put rabbit in and stir

Palm sugar in

Let it simmer away until it thickens and the meat is cooked

Just before serving add double cream

Serve with rice

Bulldog's Carbonara

Whenever I passed a supermarket, I would always pick up a cooked bacon hock from the deli! Always.

Get half the meat off the bacon hock, shred it up into bowl with 2 raw eggs

2 tablespoons of Italian grated cheese

Little glug of cream

Knob of butter

Black pepper

Cook spaghetti until just al dente

Drain it

Immediately tip it on ingredients in the bowl and stir

The eggs will cook threw with the heat of the spaghetti to make a sauce.

Rabbit Offal Breakfast

Fry livers and kidneys from the rabbit you skinned earlier!

Remember to remove the bile sack from the liver

Throw remaining bacon in from the bacon Hock

Add cream

Season with more black pepper and a pinch of salt

Serve on toast

You have died and gone to heaven.

Chicken Dinner

Exchange one England appearance

Submit expenses

Get told to fuck off

Remind yourself: Everyone Gets Fifteen Quid...

Everybody Gets Fifteen Quid is ghost-written by Tony Horne. Tony was born in Chessington, Surrey, England in 1971, attending Tiffin School for Boys in Kingston-upon-Thames, and later graduating from the University of Exeter, with a degree in French and Italian.

He also attended Rome and Padua universities in Italy. In 1990 he was runner-up in the Radio Academy's "Young Broadcaster of the 90s" competition, and has gone onto become one of the UK's most successful morning radio personalities. In August 2018, he quit professional radio full-time and now co-owns the community station, Rossendale Radio.

Alongside his radio career, he is one of the world's most in demand ghost-writers. For his subjects and his speed, he is highly recommended. His work falls mainly into the categories of crime or celebrity and include 'Save One Child' for Ian James, MBE (undercover detective bringing paedophiles to justice), 'Wildcard' for Christopher Maloney (X Factor and Big Brother), 'If Only' for Terry West (Moors Murders), 'Tango 190' for the late PC David Rathband and 'Getting Over The X' for the first X Factor winner, Steve Brookstein.

Acknowledgements

My thanks go to Mum and Dad - Joyce and John, my lovely wife Michelle and my lifelong friends where it all started, Mark and Keith Card.

Thank you also to Tom Cousins and my great touring buddy, David 'Stevo' Stevenson, Adrian and his Mum, Pat Gray, for all the driving, and the legend, Tony David. To all my friends in Ireland and America - so many great memories. You might be in the pages that follow. Gratitude also goes to the BDO and the PDC.

Finally, the last word goes to Rod Glenn at Wild Wolf Publishing and ghost-writer, Tony Horne. You will find Tony at www.tonyhornebooks.com if you need a hand writing your story.

Career

Winner

Pacific Masters

British Gold Cup

German Open

Irish Classic twice

Tramore Open

Yorkshire Classic

USA Boston Open All Three Titles Same Weekend

Kent Open twice

Sheppy Classic

Prestatyn Open

Websters Bitter Doubles Board

Florida Melbourne Open

3 X Nine Dart Legs

10 Caps For England

Runner Up

Isle Of Man Open

UK Open

World Grand Prix twice

Windy City Open

Montreal Open

Semi Final

World Championship

World Matchplay

Always room for the board in the camper

News of the World (mid-eighties)

My mate and World Champ, Tony David

First player on telly with a shaved head (it's a triceratops, by the way)

Sky headquarters with Eric and Bob

One for the pot

Taking aim!

Me and Reg at the Eastbourne Open

British God Cup Winners (me and Jane Stubbs)

The Squirrel Team, Tonbridge (dad top right)

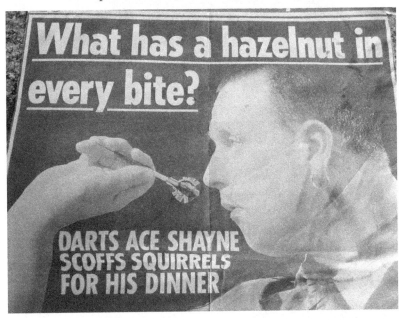

Interview in The Sun

Yes, I wore that cardigan all day

Rabbit and lager curry

A very rabbity breakfast

Jocky, my hero

Vegas in the early nineties

Me, Mark and Keith Card and Joe Tuppeny (Bullseye World
Record Attempt)

1984 World Championship tickets from Jollees Nightclub

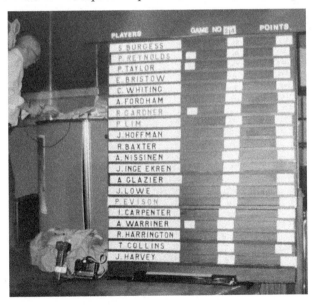

British Pentathlon and one of the rare occasions I finished above

Phil

Spanking the monkey from an early age

CPSIA information can be obtained
at www.ICGtesting.com
Printed in the USA
BVHW030927270819
556929BV00001B/19/P